David Lewis Paget was born in Nottingham, England, in November 1944. The family moved back to Staffordshire after the war, and he attended Holly Lodge Grammar School in Smethwick. It was very much cap and gown in those days, He excelled in English Language, but was rather ordinary in science subjects. His education was broken when the family migrated to Australia in 1958, and the disruption saw him leave school there somewhat disillusioned, at 15. He returned as a mature age student at 31, and completed a B.A. degree in English and History. In the meantime he had spent his twenties in the Royal Australian Air Force, studying to become an Instrument Fitter, and he served on bases in Townsville, Point Cook, Williamtown and Edinburgh, working on Neptunes, Winjeels, Mirages and Orions. It was during his service that he began to write poetry, whiling away the long hours on Duty Crew and Guard duties.

On leaving the service he taught himself offset printing, and produced a number of small volumes of poetry which were sold locally. This led to entering business as a self-employed printer, and under the name Mushroom Graphics he published a magazine called 'Traders Gate', which was distributed through the Yorke Peninsula in South Australia.

At 60 he took a teaching job for a year at the Wenzhou Medical College, Zhejiang Province, China, and wrote a number of Chinese oriented poems. He now lives in the Copper Triangle, still writing poetry.

Poems Of Myth & Scare!

by

David Lewis Paget

BARR BOOKS

For my wife,
Lynette
and my children,
Christopher, Susan, Morgan, Shea,
Blaise, Blake & Alison.

Other Poetry available by the author:

Pen & Ink — The Complete Works 1968-2008
Timepieces — The Narrative Poetry
At Journey's End — The Narrative Poetry, Vol. II
The Demon Horse on the Carousel — and Other Gothic Delights
My China — Poetry in and about China

Foreword

A lot of the poetry in this volume was written since the release of 'The Demon Horse on the Carousel – and Other Gothic Delights'. At that time I thought it might be my final collection of verse, but the muse has clung on, and I have found myself so prolific that another book is called for.

Most of these poems have not been published in book form before. Some are Gothic in theme, some are humorous, some are more philosophical. The 'Scare' part of the title comes from the fact that one Internet reviewer commented that in one out of two poems, they just knew that someone was going to end up dead. I must admit, this seems to be true. My Scorpionic nature tends to be overly morbid in respect of my fascination with death, and what comes after. For that I take a leaf from Edgar Allen Poe, who was also overly concerned with death, dying and burial practices.

The bottom line of these poems, however, is plot. Most are basically short stories in poetic form, with a strongly plotted storyline, and developed background. I try to avoid current events, as nothing dates a poem more than a factual backround of some tragedy. They are escapist in the sense that some operate in an alternative world, found only out there beyond the tramlines of suburbia. The characters are not usually the type of people you would meet in everyday life. They too have escaped in some manner or form, from normality. Why don't you join them?

David Lewis Paget   January 2013

Contents

Lady in the Mist

The day was bleak and the Tor was steep
As I walked up to the crest,
The tower of St. Michael's Church stood gaunt
And I stared, as if obsessed,
The myths lay thick on the countryside
And surrounded me as they grew,
And I hoped that I might see Avalon
By the side of the River Brue.

I thought I could hear the clash of steel
In the valley, down below,
The sound of a sword on a buckler shield
But the mist obscured the show,
The sun lay on the horizon as
It had done for a thousand years,
When Guinevere lay with Lancelot,
And she woke to her husband's tears.

I thought I'd better get off the Tor
As the light was growing dim,
The mist a-swirl in the fields below,
I'd be lost if the night set in,
I made my way down the southern slope
'Til I came to a wooden bridge,
And a lake that I hadn't seen before
From St. Michael's, up on the ridge.

Around the lake was a swampy ground
Where the reeds in profusion grew,
Climbed up the bank of the silent lake
And glistened with mist and dew,

I'd barely taken a dozen steps
On the bridge, when I heard a sigh,
And the lilting voice of a woman there
As she walked on the other side.

She was dressed in a long and trailing cloak
With a hood pulled over her face,
And she seemed to drift on the further shore
With unworldly poise and grace,
She saw me then, and she stopped and turned
And she pointed into the mere,
Where the water was only inches deep,
Then she seemed to disappear.

I rubbed at my eyes in disbelief,
I must have been seeing things,
There was nothing there but the mist, the mere
And the fear that silence brings,
I heard the jangle of armour then
And footsteps on the bridge,
But nothing to see, the bridge was clear
Though the sound had made me flinch.

I looked out over the water there
As a hand and an arm appeared,
Just where the woman had pointed to
Before she disappeared,
I seemed to see the whirling shape
Of a sword, flung into the mist,
And the hand in the lake had caught it,
Held it aloft on a slender wrist.

I blinked just once, the sword had gone,
And the lake was undisturbed,

I shook my head in confusion then
At the sight and the sounds I'd heard,
I waded into the water there
And made for the self-same spot,
I needed to satisfy myself
If the sword was there, or not!

The water was only inches deep
And clear as a crystal spring,
It didn't take me a moment there
To see what my search would bring,
An ancient sword on the surface there
That I reached on down to hold,
But found it was gripped by a skeletal hand
Wedged deep in the mud and mould.

I pulled and the bones released their grip
So I held the sword on high,
It was badly eaten away with rust
In the years it was left to lie,
Then I heard a sound on the nearer bank
And I turned to look in her face,
The woman I'd seen in the cloak and hood,
Who'd moved with unearthly grace.

She stared at me with a look sublime
But she never uttered a word,
She reached on out and I found that I
Was handing over the sword,
As she held it up, it gleamed and shone
Though her hands were bare to the bone,
Then I knew the sword was Excalibur,
It was going back to the stone.

11

She turned and drifted into the mist
Was lost in the darkening night,
I somehow knew that I couldn't go
Where the dreams and the myths unite,
She's one with the knights and Bedivere,
With Arthur, where he has gone,
To sleep in the mists of chivalry
By the waters of Avalon.

Woman in Black

'Come out, come out!' I whispered to her,
'Come out from your padded walls,
There's a world of love that waits you here,
There are hills and waterfalls,
The sky is blue in the summertime
And the swallows dive in the field,
Come out, come out,' I knocked at her door,
But the door was barred and sealed.

'You were bright and gay just yesterday,
When we walked in the park at noon,
You chattered in your excited way
Of your plans for the month of June,
You picked a posy of buttercups
And you plaited them into your hair,
Then skipped and danced as the breeze came up
For the joy of the day out there.'

'So why have you barred your door to me
When my love is fastened on you,
What has become of our reverie
That you said was more than my due?

You've locked yourself in a gloomy room
At the end of an ancient hall,
What in the world's come over you...'
'I stare at a crystal ball!'

Her voice came echoing through the door,
In the tone of a girl who'd cried,
Her sobs seeped up from the oaken floor
Of the room where she sat, inside,
'The world outside is a sham,' she said,
'The meadows are barren and dry,
And over all like a leaden pall
Is the arch of a greying sky.'

I went to say that it wasn't so
But a cloud had covered the sun,
And out beyond me the fields were dry
The river had ceased to run,
The swallows, building their nests had gone
Where the sun still shone at noon,
Shadows formed, and my face was grim
As my soul was steeped in gloom.

'What did you see in the crystal ball?'
I said, with a tongue so dry,
'I saw our love to the end of it,'
She said, and started to cry,
'I saw the woman in black that came
To shatter our marriage vow,
And tasted blood on the lip you split
That once you had kissed, 'til now.'

'That crystal ball is a lie,' I said,
'For none of it's happened yet,

13

You're looking far to a future that
My love will make you forget.'
But overhead was a thundercloud
And lightning shattered a tree,
While thunder rumbled and shook the ground
As if to admonish me.

'I'll always love you,' I shouted out,
But then it began to rain,
The thunder clattered and drowned me out,
And all I could feel was pain,
I begged my lover to let me in
But she just ignored my pleas,
And then I noticed a woman in black
Watching me through the trees!

The Valley of Dreadful Night

He hid in the fields and hedgerows,
And skirted the towns by night,
He lay in the barns of deserted farms
To sleep, when the time was right.
He always kept one step ahead
Of the pack that would hunt him down,
And stole his food in the neighbourhood
Of the cottages, far from town!

He thought of his love, his Jenny,
And gave out a savage cry,
He'd found her lying with Jack Malone
Like a pig, in a rutting sty,
He'd plunged the dagger into the heart
Of his love, and his one delight,

Then watched the fire leach out of her eyes
To the Valley of Dreadful Night!

Malone, he'd left as a warning,
His throat slit ear to ear,
No more was the great philanderer
To bed any woman here,
He propped him up at the old crossroads,
He nailed his corpse to a tree,
And left a sign: 'I was caught in crime,
Now look what's happened to me!'

His nights, they were black and broken
By dreams that troubled his sleep,
For Jenny would seem to be woken
From the depths of a bottomless creek,
She raged in his shallow nightmares,
What she said would leave him agape:
'I never loved any man but you,
It was simply a case of rape!'

Then he moaned and cried in confusion,
And he wept 'til he lay awake,
With his tear-stained face now broken,
With the loss of his heartfelt hate,
And he mourned the loss of his Jenny,
The girl with the wide, bright eyes,
And he cursed himself for a felon,
And the life that he now despised!

They found him there in the morning,
They beat, and bound him in chain,
Then dragged him off to the magistrates
As he sank in his pit of pain.

15

The judge put on the dread black cap
And thundered the words that he said:
'I have no choice but to sentence you
To be hanged by the neck, 'til dead!'

The sun, it was barely rising,
He could hear the birds from his cell,
Fluttering up in the willow tree
By the gallows, his personal hell,
They looped the rope down over his neck
And he said: 'It's only right!'
As he crashed down into a dreamless sleep
In the Valley of Dreadful Night!

The Scribe in the Woods of Time

There's an ancient wood where nobody goes
That's hid in the mists of time,
It covers a hundred miles or so
To the west of the Eden line;
The passengers on the rattling train
Will pull at the blinds, and stare,
But no-one's game to get off the train
With the howl of the wolves out there!

And the stories told of walkers, who
Have never come back to tell,
Of monstrous birds that tore at their throats,
Of blood, congealed in a well;
There are cats out there as big as goats
The snakes are draped through the trees,
And vampire bats float down in a cloud
When there's more than a passing breeze.

So none will venture into the wood
Not now, or in times gone by,
The bones that lie in the undergrowth
Are a lesson, for you and I;
But deep within is a clearing there,
A chimney that belches smoke,
A cottage door that is left ajar,
And hung on a hook, a cloak!

The cottage has stood there undisturbed
Since sixteen hundred and nine,
The man who sits at the writing desk
Is writing outside of time,
He whips up storms in the Balkans,
Conjures Thunderheads in the States,
With every swirl of his feather quill
Tornadoes twirl, or abate.

He hasn't the time to trim his beard
It curls right down to the floor,
His eyebrows droop down over his eyes,
His hair is a nest, for sure;
Where eaglets peck, and nip at his scalp,
He brushes the birds away,
And dips his quill in the ink he spills
From the blood of an old dismay!

He marshals armies across the seas,
Prefers to put them to flight,
Their weapons gone as a harsh moon shone,
The soldiers melt in the night;
He topples Princes, he topples Kings
The fate of their wives is worse,

He packs them off to the guillotine,
But he always does it in verse!

Then when the sun sinks under the rim
Of the world in its daily round,
He sits in the cottage, cloaked in gloom
And his face turns into a frown;
And he lifts his eyes to the stars above
Makes one of his heartfelt pleas:
'Allow me to scribble 'THE END', my Lord!'
But a silence rings through the trees!

Journey to Paradise

She was a queen of the old Levant,
Of a country, lost in shame,
Each page, blood-drenched of its history
Was burnt, to bury its name,
The King had gone on the last Crusade
With his knights to the Holy Land,
But locked her into a chastity belt
Forged by a blacksmith's hand.

But Queen Fatima, known as 'The Bitch'
Was a testy-tempered whore,
She raged and ranted at everyone
And chafed at the chains she bore,
She sent in search of the blacksmith to
Disable the King's device,
But word came back that the man was hung
So he'd never work it twice.

The King was away for three long years,
Fatima's tongue was a lash,
The sharpest thing in her box of tricks
Was the blade of the headsman's axe,
Her courtiers' popularity rose
And fell as her moods had bled,
And all had quaked at the first mistake
When she ranted, 'Off with his head!'

She called for a Turkic Shaman to
Divine what her life would be,
Would she ever be rid of this chastity belt?
He cautioned her, 'Wait and see!'
It wasn't the answer she wanted, so
He was tied to a horse, and dragged,
Down to the river and weighted down
Tied up in a hessian bag!

A number of fortune tellers fell
To the rage of a Fatima fit,
Off to the gory headsman's blade
Or cooked like a pig on a spit,
But then, the little court jester said
In a voice that was more like a whine,
'Would it please the ear for a genuine seer,
At Delphi, I learnt to divine.'

'You learned from the famous Oracle?
Come closer, this I must hear,
If the Oracle tells my future place,
Why, you have nothing to fear!'
'My Oracle tells the key to your belt
Has been locked in the armourer's cell,

The King had ordered its secret kept
Or he'd suffer the fiends from hell!'

They carried the armourer shackled in chain
To the queen, he knelt in shock,
'The key, if you please, or on your knees
You will feel my steel on the block!'
He babbled and begged forgiveness, said
He was caught between King and Queen,
And gave up the key to chastity
So the queen danced free on the green.

She spent that night with the eunuch slaves,
She crawled around on her knees,
She fed an insatiable appetite
Doing whatever she pleased,
At dawn she called for the headsman
Who was given his gory task,
And watched as her night companions there
Fell one and all to the axe.

She took in the jester, asked for more,
What news of the King from home,
'Alas,' he said, 'the King is dead,
The vultures pick at his bones!'
'Then what will become of his widow queen,
Say now, or you'll feel my curse.'
'A knight in armour will come for you ,
A knight on a coal black horse!'

'Will he be the bearer of tidings, or
Will he be the bearer of lies?'
'This knight has only one deed to do,
He'll bear you to paradise!'

She thought of the bliss of a loving knight
Who would take the queen as his right,
While she would rule with an iron hand
And he would make love at night.

The knight came thundering through the trees
One day, on his coal black horse,
The queen stood up where the parapet eaves
Hung over the watercourse,
She ordered the drawbridge down at once
And had the portcullis raised,
Then watched him galloping into the fort
And through the walls of the maze.

His horse came clattering up the steps
That led to milady's tower,
She thought, 'At last, we shall bed this night
In the depths of my shady bower.'
The knight, not raising his visor there
Nor even dismounted yet,
Raised his scimitar up on high
Then cleft her head from her neck!

Her body dropped like a stone, and bled,
Her head flew over the wall,
She saw his face as she stared ahead
The Jester, watching her fall,
Her head fell down through the cypress trees
And she thought that the breeze was nice!
Those final seconds would lead her mind
To the Garden of Paradise.

The Bellman

He rang it in the marketplace,
He rang it in the street,
Old Silas was the Bellman
In the village of Purfleet,
He'd rung the bell for sixty years,
He'd rung the bell for war,
He'd rung it for the harvest
But would ring the bell no more!

The Mayor and all his councillors
Had met within the Hall,
Discussed the ponderous questions
That would bear upon them all,
Their gowns were trimmed with ermine
And the mayor, he wore his chain,
The solemn Majesty of State
Was heard in their refrain!

'We must dismiss the Bellman,'
Said the hoary Abel Creep,
'He rings it at the strangest times,
I just can't get to sleep!'
'Agreed,' said Horace Fumblewit,
It's more than time enough,
I thought that he'd be dead by this…'
'Hear hear!' said Toby Gruff.

They called him to the chamber
And delivered him the score,
Old Silas staggered back in shock,
They'd rocked him to the core!

He raised the bell above his head
And gave a mighty 'Clang!'
Then jumped up on their table
Where they sat, their ears rang!

'I've been the Bellman sixty years,
My father taught me then,
His father went before him, rang
The bell for Inkerman;
But way, way back before that time
My forebears had a stake,
They warned of the Armada,
Rang the bell for Francis Drake!'

He stomped along their table
In his coarse old hob-nailed boots,
He silenced their authority
To rule in mean disputes,
For every time a councillor
Would seek to raise his voice,
The bell would drown his utterance,
It gave them little choice!

'There's been a Bellman in this burgh
Right back, before King John,
You think you petty underlings
Can rule once I am gone?
Your ancestors lie buried in
The gravel by the Church,
While mine live on in history…
I'll knock you off your perch!'

He raised the bell and made it peal,
It rocked the ancient hall,

The walls shook with vibrations
'Til the roof began to fall,
The beams came crashing down in a
Scenario from Hell,
'Your time is not forever,' cried
The man who rang the bell!

China Blue

I had seen him in the market,
I had glimpsed him in the rain,
I had tried to pick his trail up
On the Wenzhou-Hangzhou train,
Then he'd seen me drinking Kafei
In a little Shanghai Ba,
And had run the length of Nanjing Road
And fled in a jiao che.

He was Sun Peng Fei, her brother,
She was Sun Ye Ling, I knew,
But I'd always caught her smiling
When I called her China Blue,
She was sweet, and very pretty,
And I'd fallen for her, hard,
In the village school at Ping Yang
When I saw her in the yard.

We had taken to each other
And I'd tried to learn Chinese,
But she warned me of her brother,
He was grim, and hard to please,
And her parents had been angry
When they heard of me one day,

They had told her older brother
'She'll not marry a yang wei!'

At the end of the semester
China Blue had disappeared,
And I asked the Zhongwen lao shi
If it was as I had feared,
She'd been taken by her parents
And her brother to Shanghai,
Thinking I could never find her,
But I knew I'd have to try.

A needle in a haystack
Would be easier than this,
There are twenty million people
In this huge metropolis,
But I knew that I would see them
If I watched the Nanjing Road,
In that swarm of Christmas shoppers
I stayed put, and watched the crowd,

A week before that Christmas
I could see them, in a queue,
Lining up for western presents,
Mother, father, China Blue,
Then I tapped her on the shoulder
And she turned and smiled at me,
So I took her by the hand
And then I whispered 'Wo ai ni!'

'Wo ai ni,' she answered gladly
Flung her arms around my neck,
While the mother screeched at father,
And the father shook his head,

But they came with me together
And we sat in Mei Don Lao,
Where I slipped rings on her finger
And I made a solemn vow.

Then the mother, I won over,
And the father gave a grunt,
They agreed we should be married
If that's what we really want,
And the brother, he's no trouble
We go drinking, bowling too,
And I'm soon to be a father
With my love, my China Blue!

(Glossary:
Kafei – (Karfay) – coffee
Ba – (Bar) – Bar
Jiao che – (Jow Tcher) – Taxi
Peng Fei – (Peng Fay) – male name
Ye Ling – (Yer Ling) – female name
Yang wei – (yang way) – Foreign devil
Zhongwen Lao shi – (Jongwen Lao Sher) – Chinese
teacher
Wo ai ni – (war I nee) – I love you
Mei Don Lao – (May Don Lao) – MacDonalds)

Eternal Youth

I was travelling through a countryside
That I'd never seen before,
As it grew dark, the mountainsides
Loomed threatening, over my car,
The cloud hung low in a louring sky
And my headlights cut through the gloom,
Ahead on the twisting, bending road
I had hopes of a cosy room.

There wasn't a house or a farm out there,
The valley was threading down,
The deeper it went, the darker yet
With still no sign of a town,
I thought that I'd have to drive all night
And my eyes were growing dim,
When back in the trees, I saw a light
And a sign: 'The Dew Drop Inn'.

I pulled at the bell for the Publican
And I heard a shuffle inside,
A shadow loomed, and the hinges creaked
And the door swung open wide,
A man so gaunt that his face was grey
And his sallow cheeks were thin,
Stood trembling in the doorway there
In the hall of the Dew Drop Inn!'

I followed him in, not saying a word,
He motioned me into the bar,
Then poured me a whiskey and water
While I stared at a glass topped jar,

It drew my gaze as I sipped my drink
For the contents bubbled and swirled,
And I said: 'Just where is the Dew Drop Inn?'
He replied: 'At the End of the World!'

His voice came bubbling out of his chest
Like the rasp of a rusty saw,
His hands were trembling, where they lay
And he kept his eyes on the door.
'That jar, it changes its colours, look!
From red, through green and gold...'
He said: 'They told me one sip from that
And a man would never grow old!'

I stared at him, and I saw him frown
With a tear at the edge of his eye,
This ancient man with the trembling hand
And I said: 'Well, that was a lie!'
He shook his head and he turned to me
'It depends what you want it for,
I was twenty-two when I took my sip...
I'm a hundred and sixty four!'

'I didn't age for a hundred years
I revelled in youth, so long,
But suddenly I grew weary, thought
That there must have been something wrong!
I lost the zest for a youthful life,
Was beginning to feel my years,
All of my friends were dead and gone,
This life is a valley of tears!'

'You're telling me that one sip from this
Will give me a hundred - True?

I'll still be fit and I'll still be strong,
At a hundred and thirty two?'
'You will, but there's a condition
You must take on the Dew Drop Inn,
And stay in this cursèd valley then
'Til a seeker of youth walks in!'

I'm standing behind the counter with
My eyes on the outer door,
I've stood like stone for forty years
And paced a track on the floor,
The Publican left, the moment I sipped
He went with a joyous cry,
In search of a path from the Dew Drop Inn
Where at last, he could finally die!

The Eclipse

'My thoughts are often consumed by death
And the dark side of the Moon,'
I said to Jane as she sensed my pain
On that Sunday afternoon,
We'd sat through the morning sermon
Of the Tempting on the Mount,
'The Devil is often abroad,' she said,
'More times than we can count!'

'Yet God is the infinite mystery,
He never has shown himself,
He doesn't swoop down to rescue us
Or curb the excess of wealth!'
I said there were so many questions
That had led me into doubt,

29

But Jane, the waif, had a simple faith
And she turned me inside out.

'Look at the trees and bushes here
And the way they propagate,
And every species to its kind,
We're all in the hands of fate.
He works his wonders in full view
We need to open our eyes,
For his is the great creative force,'
She said, and her words were wise!

The sky had suddenly darkened
It was coming on to rain,
We dashed to the nearest clump of trees
And I reached for the hand of Jane,
I held her tight in the fading light
Sought heaven through her lips,
And fell to the leaf-strewn forest floor
Where we stayed through the sun's eclipse.

The day had become as black as night,
It was eerie, through the gloom,
As we made the wildest, passionate love
On a Sunday afternoon,
And the seed I left at the rising crest
Of our love, and the sun's eclipse,
Was the seed of the Great Creator, found
At the warmth of a woman's lips!

The Sound of the Spheres

The Rastenberg Philharmonic had sat,
Were shuffling in their seats,
And tuning their various instruments
To play '*The Survivor Suite*'.
It had only been played just once before,
They knew they were taking a chance,
The conductor and several cellists had gone
Right after *Svrili's Dance*!

One moment, the baton was waved in the air,
The next, the podium was clear,
A cellist had sawed at an awful E flat
Before he had disappeared;
Then holes had appeared in the group at the front
Where cellists and violins sat,
And all that was left of the treble bassoon
Was a sandwich, under his hat.

It wasn't as if they hadn't been warned
For Borchnik appeared on the stage,
'I scribbled this suite in a white hot heat
As I paced, in a boiling rage!
For those sitting close to the glockenspiel,
They really should cover their ears,
For once that crescendo of flute, lute and cello
Is heard - that's the Sound of the Spheres!'

Karamov turned to the audience, bowed,
Then tapped with his baton, twice,
He wouldn't be fazed to the end of his days
Though the Devil was tumbling the dice!

He looked at the fear-crazed Orchestra
Who'd heard about Borchnik's curse,
Then launched them in to *The Wages of Sin*
As an introductory verse!

The music was nothing like you would expect,
It capered and trilled, and it soared,
It spoke of the aeons of military might,
Of the soldier that fell on his sword,
The audience sat with their open jaws
As it thrilled and it burst into flight,
And carried them out where the planets sang
In a paean to endless night!

The music it raged, and the music roared
And it came to *Svrili's Dance*,
A blonde violinist took off for the door,
No way was she taking a chance!
A hole opened over a cellist's head
And swallowed the glockenspiel,
While Karamov's face went as white as the dead
When he found himself out in a field!

The Orchestra, crazed, seemed unable to stop,
The instruments sang in their hands,
The audience freaked as the piccolo peaked
And the harpsichord melted in strands,
They made for the exits in panic and fear
For the horror that waited outside,
A mammoth was leaning against the front door,
And a raptor was caught in mid-stride.

It took seven weeks for the madness to stop,
And Borchnik was run out of town,

While Karamov wanders where dinosaurs crop,
Conducting some thoughts of his own.
The Rastenberg Orchestra's now in recess,
Unlikely to play now for years,
The musicians agree that there isn't a fee
That would bring back *The Sound of the Spheres!*

The Day the Soldiers Came...

The old man sat at his cottage door
As the soldiers came to town,
And laughed as the trucks went rumbling by,
Laughed as the soldiers frowned,
They carried their rifles high that day,
Marched past him by the score,
And scowled as the old man mocked them there,
As they waged their futile war!

The tanks sat threatening in the square,
The people stood in the street,
Watching the flood of khaki power,
The boots on the marching feet,
The General stood in his jeep that day
A scroll in his scrawny hand:
'It's never too late to liberate
The folk in this tortured land!'

But then a ripple of laughter came
From the townsfolk standing there,
They seemed to enjoy a local joke,
A joke that they wouldn't share.
The soldiers were tense, bemused at that,
They'd rather the ripple of fear

They'd seen in a hundred similar towns
Since the war broke out that year.

The General barked, 'Enough of that!
Where is your National Pride?
We've come to free you from servitude
And a great deal more, beside!'
But the old man, sat in his cottage seat
Had let out a great guffaw,
And the soldiers dragged him out of his chair,
To face the General's scorn.

'Why do you laugh, old man,' he said,
'I could shoot you in your pride!'
'I'm sure you could, and probably would
As you scorch our countryside!
But what price honour, when history
Ascribes your deeds to your name,
Will shooting a poor old peasant man
Ring loud in your Hall of Fame?'

'Then why do you laugh?' the General said,
'The picture here is grim!
These soldiers fought, and died and bled,
 You lack respect for them!'
'This town has sat two thousand years,'
The old man said at last,
'Was here when Hannibal's elephants stopped
To feed on the mountain grass.'

'The Roman Legions passed through here
In their conquest and their might,
And Charlemagne's Grand Army
For a single, baleful night;

Even Napoleon Bonaparte
Conquered this little town,
For years, we had the Fascisti, and
The Nazis held us down.'

'But where have their soldiers gone today,
They lie, each under his mound,
While we sit back, as your troops attack
And thrive in our little town.
You'll only be here for a moment more
Two lines on a history page,
Just one more army to pass through here
In your arrogance, and your rage!'

The army was there for a week or so,
But then, they had to withdraw,
The old man laughed as the soldiers passed,
He let out a great guffaw;
The Rebel General brought his tanks
And a speech that he had planned:
'It's never too late to liberate
The folk in this tortured land!'

The Rain that Came to Stay

'How much longer this drought,' he said,
'The creeks are running dry,
There's not a lot in the reservoir
And not a cloud in the sky,
The farmers, shooting the cattle that
Have nothing out there to drink,
How much longer this drought,' he cried,
In the pub at Innaminck!

The soil had turned to a fine bulldust,
The drought had cracked the clay,
There wasn't a green shoot anywhere
To be seen by the light of day,
The crops had failed, were ploughed back in
In hopes that the rain would come,
But the skies were clear for the rest of the year
From there to Jerusalem!

A tinker called in a beat-up car
And staggered in with his bag,
'I'm Mickey Malone from County Down
With a thirst that could choke a shag!'
The barman served him a schooner, with
One gulp, he put it away,
But emptied his empty pockets when
The barman asked him to pay.

The tinker started his blarney then,
'I'll sharpen your knives for free!
Just give me another schooner, chum
And we'll see what we will see!
I'll cut your keys, and I'll wash a dish,
Or I'll give you a hundred pegs.'
The barman reached and he grabbed his throat,
And lifted him off his legs!

'You'll have to do better than that, my man,
You don't drink my beer for free!
I'm taking the wheels off your beat-up car
'Til you play it straight with me!'
'Hang on, hang on, just what do you want,
Whatever will pay my due!'

'We could do with a shower of rain, my man,
But that's all I'd want from you!'

The tinker nodded, 'No sooner said!
I'll make it tomorrow noon,
You'll have to give me a room to rent
And I'll whip it up in the gloom.'
The barman sneered, 'You're having me on,
No way can you make it rain!'
'You'll see, tomorrow,' the tinker said,
'Though you might think I'm insane!'

The barman locked him and his bag in a room,
And took a wheel off his car,
He knew if the tinker tried to escape
He wouldn't be going far,
But come the dawn, was a distant cloud
Spread out, and up from the south,
It tumbled and turned in the atmosphere
And looked like a dragon's mouth.

At noon the cloud was over their heads,
All black, and threatening rain,
A whirly blew up a dust storm there
And swirled at each window pane,
They locked the door of the pub up tight
And waited, tense as a rag,
The rain came down, 'Aha,' he said,
And the tinker patted his bag!

The patter of rain was heard on the roof,
The gutters began to fill,
The windows washed of their dust and silt
Right down to the window-sill,

The dust was settled, the ground was wet,
The cattle lowed in the field,
And everyone danced in the yard out there
The tide of their fortunes sealed.

The rain grew heavier by the hour,
The creeks had started to flow,
And even the reservoir burst its banks,
With nowhere else to go,
The water flooded across the plain
They waded up to their knees,
'Enough, enough!' But Malone replied:
'Begorra, you're hard to please!'

It rained all night, and the following day,
It rained and rained for a week,
The pub was flooded from wall to wall
The water burst from the creek,
'You've got to stop it,' the barman cried,
But the tinker stood and frowned,
'If the water rises much higher than this,
I think that we'll all be drowned!'

'You said you wanted the rain, all right,
I gave it, now for my pay,
I can't go on in these tattered clothes
And my car's a give-away.
I'll need the van that you've parked out front
And a hundred cans of beer,
Not much to ask for your water, chum,
At the drought time of the year!'

The barman collared and kicked him out
With his bag and all beside,

The tinker lay in the water there,
His bag had sunk in the tide,
'Will you stop it now,' the barman said,
'Or you'll wish you'd never been born!'
I can't!' The tinker sat and he cried,
'You've drowned my Leprechaun!'

It rains and rains at Innaminck,
It rains both day and night,
The pub sank under the water there
In a lake that's ten miles wide,
The farmers had to desert the land
To leave their sunken homes,
But put out a 'Wanted', Nation wide
For a tinker, called Malone!

The Castle of Lost in Time

The Castle that stood in the farmer's field
Was a grey and battered shrine,
As kids we'd clamber the battlements
And imagine a former time,
When Norman soldiers stood at the heights,
Looked down on the Saxon serfs,
Who paid their tax to the Baron there
When the Normans ruled the earth!

And I'd be Baron Fitzwulf up there,
While Craig would be Robin Hood,
Our histories would be twisted there,
We'd mix and match what we could.
A hundred years was a slip of time
To pray for my own soul's sake,

When I was Thomas A'Becket, and
He was Sir Francis Drake.

The walls were battered and falling down
Had been since the Cromwell siege,
When Charles had fled with his standard, said
No longer to be 'My Liege!'
The cannon had ripped through the southern wall
Had brought the portcullis down,
And the Roundheads, ferried across the moat
Had slain every man they found!

But ivy clung to the stubborn stone,
And climbed right up to the tower,
Where knights once practised their courtly love
Grew the strangest sort of flower,
Its petals red in the morning sun
With a heart of gold within,
'They'd pluck it up on their lances there,'
Said Craig, 'for Ann Boleyn!'

Above our heads was a fireplace
Set high in the ancient wall,
The beams long gone where a floor belonged,
There'd once been a stately hall,
Where Dames had danced in their silken gowns
And knights had cast in their lots,
Had drawn up the Magna Carta there
For the shame of John the fox!

But Farmer Giles was a bitter man
And he'd chase us over the brook,
Whenever he showed in the Castle grounds,
No matter what time it took,

He even managed to fence it off
But we'd scale the fence with glee,
And play to our hearts content, with him
Away where he couldn't see!

One night, we carried our sleeping bags
And stole through the darkening night,
I was the Duke of Marlborough
And Craig was Sir Hugh De'Spight,
We made our way through the ruins, found
A nook, we could safely sleep,
'We'll wait 'til the morning light,' I said,
'Then we'll play the Lord of the Keep!'

We woke as the Moon beamed overhead
Peeked out through a glowering cloud,
I could hear the strains of a harpsichord
The murmured sounds of a crowd,
A man that looked like a villainous lord
Appeared, not saying a word,
We scrambled out of our sleeping bags
As he drew out a wicked sword!

Then Craig took off with a yell, and I
Flew over the slated floor,
We jumped down into a passageway
That hadn't been there before,
The walls were damp with an evil stain
And brands that flickered the way,
Along to the castle dungeons, filled
With chains, and a smell - Decay!

And there in a tiny cell we saw,
Most rivetting sight of all,

The skull of a grinning skeleton,
Chained fast to the dungeon wall,
The bones were covered in cobwebs
But he'd scrawled in dust on the floor,
'Pray God to smite all mine enemies,
The Devil will take them all!'

We heard the clanking of chains along
The darkened passageway,
And like a shroud in a shimmering cloud
Was a soldier, dressed in grey,
His stare was that of a madman, crazed
The fires of hell in his eyes,
As he seized the haft of a burning brand
He looked like the Farmer, Giles!

I ran clean through the spectre, thought
That Craig was coming behind,
Cleared the end of the tunnel, leapt
Back up in a single bound,
I didn't stop for a backward glance
I ran with a sense of doom,
Away from the Castle of Lost in Time
To the safety of my room.

I never saw Craig, my friend again,
They scoured the countryside,
Ravaged the ancient Castle grounds,
Questioned me 'til I cried!
They found him dead in the dungeon
Chained, and lying against the wall,
A piece of flint in a bloodied hand
That had scraped in a childish scrawl:

'May the Devil smite him, through and through,
Mine enemy, Sir Giles FitzHugh!'

The Coven

I had shot a couple of pheasants,
Was returning, deep from the wood,
Avoiding the crackle of branches, making
As little noise as I could,
The sky was clear and a harvest moon
Shone down through the old oak leaves,
When I saw the glimmer of candlelight
Shimmering through the trees.

I hid myself by the mighty oak
That had grown, six hundred years,
And heard the mutter of chanting there,
The rhyme of an evil verse,
I looked on out to a clearing where
The Devil and all were stood,
Thirteen candles and thirteen cloaks
And thirteen wearing a hood.

The Devil stood on an ancient stump
His face was hid from the mass,
He held a crucifix upside down
They all bowed down in the grass,
A woman rose from the group and peeled
The cloak that covered her form,
The sight of her beauty caught my breath
As if I'd never been born!

The hood remained, and concealed her face
As she dropped down on all fours,
The Devil leapt from his stump, and raged,
Then took her there by force;
The others chanted and danced about
In a circle, for some rite,
Despoiling the Devil's chosen witch
Was the purpose of that night.

They all dispersed as the moon went in
Was hid by an ugly cloud,
I kept my eye on the Devil's form
He was wrapped in a purple shroud,
I trailed him, loping, out of the wood
Like a beast that's held at bay,
And brought him struggling to the ground
To see what he'd have to say.

I ripped the hood from his evil face,
He snarled and snapped in the night,
'Let's have a look at those evil eyes!'
He growled, and put up a fight;
But I laid him low by the mansion gate
And I held him there on the ground,
He yelled: 'I'm the Lord of Leighton Hay
The Lord of these these woods and downs!'

'So this is the Demon Devil's face,
Then who was the Winsome Witch?
I'm sure the Lady of Leighton Hay
Would be ready to flay the bitch!'
'You mustn't tell, it would break the spell
Of the coven, and all my power,
What would you take for your silence, now,
For the reck of this parlous hour!'

'There's just one thing that I'd take from you
To silence this gossiping tongue,
She's sweet, petite, and has dancing feet,
And I guess you know, she's young!'
'If you mean the Lady Caroline,
My daughter, never for you!'
'Oh well, the Lady of Leighton Hay
May brew up a Hell of a stew!'

That was a year and a day ago,
We wed, and live in the lodge,
The witches are still in the woods out there,
I often go out to watch;
But my Lady wife is an innocent,
I know she'd never deceive,
Except for the pot of serpents and frogs
She brewed on All Hallows Eve!

Death Whispers in My Ear

The doctors said: 'Take her away,
There's nothing we can do,
The life is seeping from her blood
Her soul is weeping too,
But keep her in a darkened room
And hidden from the light,
Perhaps you'll gain a week or two
Before her soul takes flight!'

I drove her to 'The Grange' at that,
Post haste, in coach and four,

I veiled her in black crepe and lace,
She fainted at the door.
I carried her, she was so slight
I feared she might be dead,
And laid her on the davenport
A pillow at her head.

I covered her with red damask
And drew the velvet drapes,
There'd be no light for her again
This side of heaven's gates,
She stirred in her delirium
And sighed with every tear,
'Once you were mine, but now I find
Death whispers in my ear!'

I lit a single candle, and
The beam fell on her face,
Though she was *in extremis* she
Had lost but little grace,
If only she had looked at me
To whisper words of love,
But he was near, Sir Ralph de Vere,
And ruled her from above.

He'd lured her from our marriage bed
And had his way with her,
He'd dazzled her with sweet perfumes
And trinkets by the score,
He'd danced her off her pretty feet
And turned her face from me,
And like a fool, I fought a duel
With aristocracy.

Two pistols primed, he turned and fired
But most erratically,
His Second begged to cease it there
But I aimed carefully,
My first had pinged his shoulder
But he stood his ground, and stared,
The second bullet, true and straight
Left Ralph de Vere quite dead!

The Seconds swore it legal when
The Magistrate was called,
But not so my Elizabeth;
No! - She was quite appalled.
She sank into a stupor there
Of shock and binding grief,
'You've taken all my love,' she cried,
'You're just a petty thief!'

A week she lay within these walls
A week of no respite,
I heard some ghostly mutterings
Around The Grange at night,
And then an apparition formed
Beside that davenport,
That wraithlike Peer, Sir Ralph de Vere
That I had set at naught.

The wraith leant over where she lay,
Held out a bony hand,
She rose up from the davenport
And laughed that she could stand,
They drifted from that hateful room,
Where I would have to stay,
Her body on the davenport
They faded both away.

I paced about that fateful night
And raged there in the gloom,
Her stolen soul had taken flight
From dearth, within that room.
And now I find my nightly plight
Is worse than dreamless fear,
Its bony hands caught at my throat,
Death whispers in my ear!

The Tryst

Ambrose stood at the cottage step
A bouquet in his hand,
He'd come to woo sweet Adeline
From a strange and far off land,
They'd known each other since children, and
They'd made to each a vow:
'I never will love another more
Than I love you, even now!'

They'd played in the heat of the summer sun,
They'd played in the autumn shade,
But winter carried him far from home
And the love that they'd almost made,
They wrote through spring and the summer's height
They wrote right through to the fall,
But the winter chills saw the postman fill
No letterbox at all.

His letters came back, duly stamped
'Not known at this address!'
He grieved as the spring made true love sing
Anew in his sorrowing breast,

He bought a ticket and travelled home
Third Class, by Packet Steam,
But fretted all of the way across
For the love of his Adeline.

He knocked at the cottage door where she
Had lived when the world was good,
But the knocker made an echoing sound
On the door, where Ambrose stood,
The flowers she'd tended lovingly
Were dead in the window box,
Except for a patch of colour there,
A clump of forget-me-nots.

He knocked, and then he knocked again,
There came no patter of feet,
Only the sound of silence there
As he felt his own heart beat,
He little knew as he turned away
That a bier stood in the hall,
And the coffin that lay there sombrely
Knew nothing of life at all.

She'd ceased to write when she caught the sight
Of the blood on her handkerchief,
And the winter cough said clear enough
That there'd be no summer heat,
She lay in the coffin, sweetly dressed,
With a note beside her brow:
'I never will love another more
Than I love you, even now!'

The Cavalier

He'd wandered into the party through
The French Doors, facing the lake,
Was vague, and missing a bob or two,
Perhaps he'd made a mistake?
Taken a left at the crossroads where
The kids had hidden the sign,
Instead of a right to the Graham's house,
I'd ask him, given the time.

The party was getting out of hand
The punch was spiked with gin,
And vodka and tequila and…
God knows what else was in!
For Jane was down to her underwear
While Pat fell down in a heap,
And Margaret danced on the table while
Her kids were sound asleep.

The clock in the hall struck midnight then
And I was getting tired,
I went on the hunt for Carolyn,
I thought that she'd expired,
But there she was, in the corner with
The stranger in the hat,
A funny thing with a feather in
And fancy dress, at that.

I thought that I'd introduce myself,
I'd not seen him before,
Perhaps he worked at the agency,
I'd ask, she'd know the score,

But Carolyn acted nervous when
I tried to hold her hand,
'What gentleman is this, I pray?'
He asked of Carolyn.

'Oh Phil, he's simply a husband,'
She replied, she was sublime,
I note she mentioned 'a husband' but
No mention that 'He's mine!'
'And what are these folk that prate, disport
And act themselves remiss,
Is he from the Long Parliament?
God help him, if he is!'

I knew the punch had been tampered with
But he hadn't been there long,
Maybe he'd savoured something else,
Who knew what he was on!
But Carolyn gave me that funny look
And I edged back into the room,
Leaving the two of them talking there
In the corner, in the gloom.

We'd always had an arrangement, she
Had friends, and I had mine,
We never questioned each other, and
We found that it worked out fine,
She'd spend a night on the town or so
And fix me up a tray,
While I'd go visiting Annabel
For a tumble in the hay.

We'd purchased the house at Kineton,
When she'd said: 'It has such charm!'

And I was content to be out there
In the country, near a farm,
They said the place was historic
Dating back to the civil war,
But not 'til the night of the party
Did I give it a second thought.

By one, the following morning, when
The party was winding down,
I found that Carolyn disappeared
With the stranger to the town,
She sent me a mobile message, 'Will
You come and get me, Phil?
I'm right in the heart of a skirmish
Down the slope, just by Edgehill!'

I drove to the ancient battlefield
In the dark, on a Moonless night,
But nothing stirred in the field out there
In the beam of the car's headlight,
My phone lit up with another call
And her voice came drifting through,
'My God, I'm stuck in a battle, Phil,
In 1642!'

She'd taken off with the Cavalier,
I knew what he was by now,
A straggler caught in the folds of time
That had fetched up here, somehow,
And Carolyn faded into the past
As she'd made it more than clear,
I'm the only man with a wife that ran
Away with a Cavalier!

Big Mack

I have always been a trucker
I was raised on diesel fumes,
And I smoked two packs of Lucky's
From daybreak to afternoons,
While I ate at roadside café's
From a plate that swam in grease,
And I downed two mugs of coffees
In my cab, the one I leased.

My Big Mack, my eighteen-wheeler
That I drove through western plains,
Then I hauled pigs out of Denver
And I hauled freight into Maine,
And I kept my eyes wide open
As I popped those purple hearts,
I could feel my heart keep pounding
As I rolled beneath the stars.

It's a great and grand old country
From New York to Idaho,
From the Rockies to Vancouver
And then down to Mexico,
And I've seen Tornado Alley
With a twister coming down,
And then through Louisiana
Where I've stopped, and gone to ground.

I was hauling hogs to Houston
Eighteen hours on the clock,
I was five hours past the limit so
I couldn't fill my Log,

And the Bears were getting furry
On the highway, going down,
I was too much in a hurry,
Took the rig the back way round.

It was getting on for midnight
And the night was more than black
As I found the off-road highway was
Just nothing but a track,
There were headlights in the distance
So I pulled off to the side,
Thought I'd wait for them to pass me
On that long and lonely ride.

But the lights approached me slowly
Then just pinned me in their beam,
And I squinted through the darkness
Not believing what I'd seen,
For the 'truck' that sat before me
Let out grunts and whirrs and squeals,
And I couldn't help but notice
That this 'truck', it had no wheels.

I sat frozen in my cabin
As this thing began to glow,
And it raised itself above me
Lit me up there, down below,
Then the eighteen-wheeler lifted
And without the slightest sound,
I was up there in the darkness
In the air, and looking down.

It could well have been a twister
Picked me up and flung me round,

I have seen whole trucks in twisters
Lifted up, clean off the ground,
But this thing that was above me
Took me on some drunken ride,
Skimming trees and fertile pastures
Shallow lakes and mountainsides.

It was some hallucination
From the pills I'd popped that day,
It was my imagination
Well I thought so, anyway;
But the cabin door flew open
And I leant out, looking down,
This was no imagination,
I was miles above the ground.

I slammed the door and took a slug
Of bourbon, my Jim Beam
That I'd hidden in the cabin,
All it did was make me dream,
With pills, it must have knocked me out
I crashed out in the cab,
And didn't wake 'til morning
Frozen stiff, and feeling drab.

The Mack sat to its axles in
A field of pearl white snow,
A farmer looking up at me,
And willing me to go,
I asked him where I was and then
I phoned the base, back home:
'He said that I'm in Greenland!
How I got here, I don't know!'

I smoke three packs of Lucky's
Sometimes four, it all depends,
On whether I've passed out on Beam,
I'm not one to pretend,
I haven't been inside a rig
That night is with me still,
I never drive at night, and Hey!
I bet I never will!

The Love that Binds

My father died of the cholera
In eighteen thirty-two,
There wasn't a place at the cemetery
To bury him, that we knew,
The signs were posted at Netherton,
'Don't bring your bodies here!'
The Sexton spoke: 'Try Gospel Oak,
Or maybe, Wednesbury.'

We loaded Pa back onto the cart
And whipped the old grey mare,
We'd not long buried our cousin Jack
At the turning of the year,
From Manchester to Birmingham
The epidemic spread,
From Liverpool to Leeds, to York,
With one in twenty dead!

I walked along with the horse and cart
And I passed so many more,
They thrust their relatives out, feet first
In front of the tradesman's door,

The fear had spread so rapidly
No family was safe,
So Grandma went in her winding sheet
Outside, with her Sister Kate!

They loaded bodies onto a cart
No dignity in death,
And piled them three and four feet high
As they took their final breath,
And pits were dug as the space grew less
The Churchyards all were full,
For years, the gardeners turned them up
Old bones, and a grinning skull!

We took our Pa on home at last
With nowhere else to go,
And sat him out in the potting shed
Where the seedlings used to grow,
Then Ma sat down beside him there
And died of a broken heart,
We knew it would be a waste of time
To break out the horse and cart.

For years they sat untouched out there
Through spring and the summertime,
I looked one day, they were overgrown
With a creeper, like a vine,
The vine had woven in and around
Through bones that were falling apart,
It tied and bound them together,
Wrapping a tendril round each heart.

'When things calm down, we'll bury them,'
I said to my brother, Sid,

As time went on, we both forgot
And I guess we never did;
They're closer now than they were in life
She doesn't scold or moan,
While he clings fast to his silent wife,
And at least, they're both at home!

The Grail

In the village Bellastrino
On the craggy Tuscan hills,
Lies an old abandoned Abbey
And the Church of San Michele,
Though the village was abandoned
There are two who would not go,
The Abbot, Father Grandier,
The Priest, Don Angelo.

The Abbey on the mountain top,
The Church down in the dell,
They'd fought, these two, for twenty years
Consigning each to Hell!
For in the Church of San Michele
Before the village failed,
Down in the crypt, beneath the floor
They'd found the Holy Grail.

A bowl, fine wrought in pale green glass,
There's no room for debate,
The Templar Knights had left it in
Eleven eighty-eight,
They'd always said they would return,
In fact, they never did,

They went to challenge Saladin
And died, as they had lived!

'It's mine,' said Father Grandier,
'Not so,' said Angelo,
'I found it and I'm keeping it,
Here, in the Church below.'
'It should be in the Abbey,'
Father Grandier opined,
'Its glory on the mountain top…'
'Not so! The Grail is mine!'

For years the two had tussled
Had approached the Holy See,
The Pope thought it ridiculous
And said: 'Don't bother me!
We have two dozen of those things,
A heap of rusty nails,
All from the Cross at Calvary
But these are peasant tales.'

A Cardinal then came to call
And tried to sort them out,
Well practiced in diplomacy
He said: 'No need to shout!
You have a choir each,' he said
'Who visit in the spring,
So hold a competition here,
What better way, than sing?'

'The better choir shall win the Grail
And keep it for a year,
Up in the Abbey's mountain top,
Or down here, if you dare.

Then sing for it each passing year,
Three judges, understood?
If one should win it three years straight
They keep the Grail for good!'

With many muttered mumblings
And hellfire in their eyes,
The Abbot and the priest said yes,
Dissembled with their lies,
They each set out to cheat their way
To keep that Holy Grail,
The Abbot got to pick each judge
He thought he couldn't fail!

The Abbey won the first two years
And held the Grail on high,
While poor Don Angelo despaired,
The time was coming nigh;
They had to sing for it once more,
He knew that if he failed,
The Abbot would, victorious,
Not let him keep the Grail.

Don Angelo went down to Rome
And brought a tenor back,
His voice like rich red Tuscan wine
To join his choir's attack,
They sang their hearts out on the day
But saw the judges feign,
And shake their heads, Don Angelo
Had nothing left to gain.

The judge stood up to name the prize,
The Abbot had his way,

The tenor stood and sang a note
Not heard since Jesu's day,
He held it long, unwavering
The Grail began to ring,
A long high-pitched reverberance,
The Grail began to sing.

A minute there, without a breath
The tenor held his tone,
And Grandier stood up, alarmed,
Let out a fervid moan,
The Grail sang on, then shattered
Fell in pieces to the floor,
The judge stood up and shook his head,
Then said – 'The sing's a draw!'

The Abbey holds the base of it,
Up on the mountain top,
All glued together, like some vase
Bought in the Red Cross Shop.
While down there in the little Church
On a thousand Euro tips,
They're coining them a fortune with
The rim that touched his lips!

The Castle in the Marsh

The Castle out in the marshes ruled
The serfs with an iron rod,
The yeomen, hidden in cottages,
Were careful where they trod,
The soldiers poured from the Castle walls
And rode the peasants down,
They stole the women they caught abroad
And returned to the Castle grounds.

There was only a single causeway that
Was guarded, night and day,
Many a father came to grief
When crossing the moat, to pay,
To save his daughter from certain shame,
A fate that, worse than death,
Was tearing the heart from Amber Vale
As the mothers mourned, distressed.

The Baron, Ralph Fitzherbert held
His acres from the King,
(That William, known as Rufus, who
Would hunt most anything),
He was known as 'Baron Slaughter'
For he murdered them at will,
He burdened them all with taxes,
Raped and pillaged, and then he'd kill.

The women held in the Castle Keep
Were set to work, and raped,
They scrubbed in the kitchen galley, cooked
The food, and cleaned the grate,

Two of their number were trusted to
Go out in the misty marsh,
Collecting the herbs and mushrooms for
The Captain of the Guard.

But Aethelflaed had been pregnant with
Fitzherbert's only son,
She came to term in the August and
She hated everyone:
'The boy's as good as a Norman, I'm
The wife of a Saxon squire,'
She wept, and then she had strangled it,
Throwing it in the fire!

Fitzherbert ranted all day long,
Lamenting what she'd done,
'I should have known that a Saxon whore's
Not fit to bear my son!'
He stripped and flayed 'til the flesh had peeled,
'Til he thought that his arm would tire,
Then dragged her over the hearth, and placed
Her hands in the blazing fire!

They hung her naked from a tree
As the villagers came to wail,
Then rode and murdered her husband there
In the village of Amber Vale,
The women held in the Castle wept
At the Normans' cruelty,
They'd whisper: 'That was Aethelflaed,
But it might as well be me!'

The Baron held a feast that night
And they drank of their Norman wine,

From casks brought in from Normandy
But opened before they dined,
By midnight they were vomiting
Were helpless, caught in a trance,
From the berries of deadly nightshade squeezed
As the women began to dance.

They lopped off every soldier's head
As they lay, none thought it harsh,
Then they bound and carried the Baron out
And thrust him into the marsh,
With an apple jammed in his gaping jaw
And his glaring eyes so big,
He sank 'til his head was all they saw
Like the head of a slaughtered pig.

The trees at Amber Vale were hung
With a strange but exotic fruit,
The heads of the soldiers hanging there
With their coats of mail, to suit,
They stormed the Castle and burnt it down
The ruins would make you quail,
For Belladonna is nurtured there
By the village of Amber Vale!

The Book

It was late in the autumn of 2210
The shuttle had gone off to Mars,
The highways of Asia were solidly blocked
With a billion Chinese cars,
I'd wandered around the Museum of Trees,
The Fruit Section opened my eyes,
The bitterness taste of electronic apples
So cleverly changed, and disguised.

I seemed to be wandering round on my own,
Museums were on their way out,
The Virtual Channels were simple to screen
And more easy to access, no doubt.
The ancient attendant had followed me round,
He warily started to say:
'I have something hidden, way out in the back
If you're interested, come out this way!'

He led to a room that was dingy and dark,
Went over and pulled up the blind,
The place was so dirty, with cobwebs and dust,
'Not used much; I hope you don't mind!'
And there on the table he pointed it out,
A thick slab of something - I looked,
'You'll not see another of these in your life,
'What is it?' I said. 'It's a book!'

He lifted the thick leather cover for me,
To show what he called was a page,
'The government banned them in '73,
They said they caused people to rage.

We're not used to words on a scale such as this…'
There were words and more words, like a plague,
They dazzled my vision, I staggered a bit
Like a man who is struck with an ague.

He turned other pages, a hundred of them,
A thousand, I just couldn't count,
And every one teeming with words on each page
So the figures continued to mount.
'We're used to see just fifteen words in a line,
We twitter and tweet all the time,
How could a person sit down with a book
With all that! - without blowing his mind?'

'It's called 'General Knowledge', the old man replied,
'Not something you hear every day,
And fabulous stories and verses in rhyme,
And the glory of history's sway.
There once was a time, there were millions of these,
Each home had a shelf full of books,
But once our technology grabbed at our minds
We were lost, we were pretty well hooked!'

'The government knew it was dumbing us down,
You can't fight what you'll never know,
By banning the books and the Libraries
Our minds were beginning to slow.'
I left there quite thoughtful, I needed to write
How misled we had been, and were blind,
I started with paper, a pen and some ink
And believe it! - I wrote it in rhyme!

Voice in the Wind

I could hear her whispering under the trees
Whenever the breeze crept in through the pines,
And then when the Moon rose out of the sea
It soughed and it sifted out from the vines,
I'd stop and I'd listen, straining to hear
What the voice would sigh in the bright green sedge,
'Ah me!' it started, then faded away,
Went searching for dreams at the water's edge.

I'd follow it down through the rocks and pools
As the tide swept in, and over my feet,
Down where the crabs and the lobsters ruled
A ledge that was straddled by Neptune's seat.
The tremulous voice in the runnels there
Was inarticulate, ravaged with pain,
But the breakers crashed, and they drowned it out
When I called for the creature's name, in vain.

But back in the shack on that lonely shore
Where I'd fled to, after the accident,
And lying awake I could hear the roar
Of the crash, the train where the tracks were bent,
And Jill was alive in my mind, alight
As she'd whispered, just as we overturned:
'I want you to know that I'm yours tonight,
Though the stars have fallen, the heavens burned!'

Each morning I'd stare at the plaster wall
But thinking of nothing, my mind a blank,
I wouldn't go anywhere else at all,
The funeral church had been dark and dank.

Her father had hated the sight of me,
The mother had blamed for her daughter's life,
They'd pushed us together, couldn't they see?
She hated them both and had paid the price!

My world is haunted by shades from the past
My future has limited time to play,
I hear a whisper arise from the sea
At the end of every gruelling day.
I hear the whisper and know it's Jill,
Her spirit is free in the fading light,
I know what she's saying, whispering still:
'I want you to know that I'm yours tonight!'

The Witches of Little Begone

Little Begone was a tiny place
Untouched by the fronds of time,
The cottages there, since Edward the third
Had lain in a valley sublime,
Wisteria climbed at the cottage walls
Where lilies and lilacs grew,
And over a fence, the witches stared,
In Little Begone there were two.

They hated each other in Little Begone,
The youngest was Annabel Prank,
She'd stolen the seeds of a magical herb
From the garden of old Mother Skank,
So Skank put a spell on her garden that
Instead of the herbs, would grow
An army of huge zucchini's that
Would spread, right into the road.

Annabel tried to dig them out
But they seemed to grow and grow,
'That will teach you to mess with me,'
Old Mother Skank had crowed.
So Annabel stormed back into the house
And put on her witches hat,
She turned Skank's cat to a cockerel,
And her cockerel into a cat!

Skank didn't know 'til the cock miaowed
And the cat began to crow,
'I've more spells than you know about,'
She screamed from the path below,
She sent an army of ugly toads
To breed in her neighbour's pond,
While Annabel watched the zucchini's grow
And sank in a deep despond.

That night she summoned up Beelzebub
While Skank sat down to plot,
Set fire to her neighbour's chimney piece
And shattered the chimney pots,
So Skank called up an army of bats
To nest in her rival's eaves,
When Annabel ran, with bats in her hair
Skank followed her through the trees.

They fought, pulled hair, and scratched and screamed
'Til the neighbour's all came out,
'Isn't it time that we ducked these two,'
Said the blacksmith, Simon Stout.
They seized and carried them down to the pond
And they brought the ducking chair,

Then ducked them both, and they both came up
With pondweed in their hair.

'If you don't behave in Little Begone
Begone is what you'll be,
We've had enough of your witch's tricks
Since fifteen forty three!'
Now Annabel sells zucchini's at
The market, by the bank,
And she always looks the other way
When she spots old Mother Skank!

The Grave that I Dug for You!

It was three o'clock in the morning
On the final day of spring,
I was stuck in a hole in the graveyard
Of Saint Matthews, Nether Ling,
I like to dig them at nightfall when
The folk are home, in bed,
Not wandering round the churchyard
Making a racket, waking the dead!

It's creepy enough as it is, whenever
The Moon sails over the church,
And shines its beams on the headstones
Of Jack Dervish, or Bill Burch,
Of mad old Widow Maloney, who,
The stories do abound,
Was carried kicking and screaming
In her coffin, and put in the ground.

My job is a labour of love, I've lived
In this village, all my life,
I know each one who lives here, every
Mistress, husband and wife,
Whenever I dig a grave, I know
Exactly who it's for,
And shed the bitter, parting tear
For the ones who go before.

I've even dug for my own, my
Darling mother, and my dad,
They left on that last long journey when
I was but still a lad,
The Vicar made me the Sexton, so
That I could earn my keep,
Living alone in the cottage, ghosts
Would haunt me in my sleep.

I often manage an extra grave,
That I dig by the iron fence,
All overhung with the creepers, that
I buy, for Peter's Pence,
They're there for the poor and needy who
Can't manage a burial fee,
So I carry the bodies at midnight, drop
Them in, all buried for free!

I always attend the services,
And stand right up at the back,
And that's where I first saw Caroline,
My love, my Caroline Black,
She went to her brother's funeral
With veil, and covered in lace,
But the wind blew up as she left, and then
I saw sweet Caroline's face.

71

I fell; I saw and was smitten,
She had given me half a smile,
I felt so bold as to ask her if
I could walk with her, for a while.
We went some way, she held my hand
And she looked me, square in the eye,
'What would you say if I told you that
My mother's about to die?'

It seemed that her mother had cancer,
So she told me, with a tear,
They'd told her mother three months ago
She wouldn't live out the year,
She lived way up on the hillside there
In the mansion called 'Beau Clair',
I thought that she must have money
But she said - 'The cupboard is bare!'

The money they'd paid for the funeral
Of her brother had been the last,
Her father had gone some years ago,
And had left them little cash,
'How will I bury my mother,' Caroline
Cried, as women will do,
'Now don't you fret,' I assured her,
I have a grave I've dug for you!'

The mother died the following week,
The doctor had thought it strange,
He'd given the mother a bill of health
To last to a ripe old age,
The coroner was quite upset
When he found how the woman died,

It seemed the autopsy findings showed
Her full of insecticide.

The brother was raised at once, I know,
I dug him up in the night,
Surrounded by Sheriff's officers
Who carried a lantern light,
They found the same insecticide
Had seeped right into his bones,
And Caroline went on trial that day
In spite of her sobs, and moans.

I saw her once, right after the trial
When the judge put on his hat,
That little black square of portent
That had sentenced Caroline Black.
He'd said: 'You shall be hanged by the neck,
Pray God for your soul to save,
Your crimes are the crimes of parricide,
They will follow you, into the grave!'

They let me into the holding cell
As she waited to be sent down,
So pale and brave now the deed was done
Though she kept her eyes on the ground.
'If only…' I had begun to say,
But she stayed me: 'What can you do?'
'I can keep you warm, and comfortable,
In the grave that I dug for you!'

The Exodus

I think it began with the airline strike,
No planes, not in, nor out,
The pilots didn't know who to blame,
'Not us,' they said, 'old Scout!'
'It must be a Union thing,' they said,
But then the trains had stopped,
And the truckies set their trucks in a ring
That the diesel tax be dropped.

A city of half a million
Where everyone stayed at home,
Petrol ran out at the bowsers, so
There was nowhere left to roam,
'It could only happen in Westernport,
This City of the Damned,'
The people moaned, and the airwaves groaned,
And the Internet was jammed.

People were phoning the government
But they weren't returning calls,
The Mayor had gone on a golfing trip,
They said, to Cedar Falls,
The 'News' had run out of newsprint
By the end of the second week,
So the paper stands were empty, and
The Internet was weak.

The ISP's said sorry, but
Our Networks are closing down,
There's been some trouble with hackers
From some place in another town,

The radio went on the blink
And the TV screens were snow,
The people gathered on pavements
Wandering round, no place to go!

The blackout lasted another week,
Then the city's power failed,
The engineers had scratched their heads,
'We have to get this nailed!'
But then the water had stopped its flow
Through half a million pipes,
And the fear in the city began to grow
As thieves took over the night.

Before the strike, the news had been
That the Yanks were back in space,
Right back up there with the Russkies
With the Chinese, saving face,
They'd each gone on an exploring binge,
The Yanks had gone to Mars,
While the Russkies tackled Saturn, and
The Chinese, out to the stars.

We'd heard no more, the airwaves dead
With just the noise from space,
Crackling through transistors as
More women carried Mace,
When Sunday morn, on the fourth weekend,
They got a genny fired,
Pedalling on an ancient bike,
Tooks turns, until they tired,

There was just enough for a laptop, though
Its batteries had been flat,

They brought a flickering picture up
To see where they were at,
They hooked it up to a satellite
And they called up Google Earth,
And ranged the view wherever they could,
But all they found was dearth.

The land lay waste on continents
That had housed a billion souls,
The cities and towns were quiet, as if
The people had turned to trolls,
America was a vacant place
While Europe lay serene,
And even the seas had ceased to move,
Not a breaker to be seen!

We live in the city of Westernport
The City of the Damned,
There isn't a thing alive out there,
No man to till the land,
And people are starving in the streets,
I think we can't go on...
'But what has become of the human race?'
'They disappeared! They're gone!'

Ghost Train

We were off to visit the Carnival,
Me, George and Julie Anne,
George was our mother's boyfriend,
(Though in fact, he was a man!)
I was seven and Julie six
And our Mum waved us goodbye,
She said she had some shopping to do
Told Julie not to cry!

George looked up to the heavens with
His fake, long-suffering grin,
For Julie cried a helluva lot,
She couldn't keep it in,
He took us down on the bus that night
There wasn't room to park,
The evening stars were coming out
It was getting kinda dark.

We saw the lights of the Carnival
And Julie's face lit up,
There were lots of rides and coconut shies
And Julie rode in a duck,
While George and I on the rifle range
Picked off some metal bears,
That raced across at the back, stood up,
Then fell to the pellets there.

There were clowns and men with megaphones,
And Chili Dogs with cheese,
And plenty of fluffy candy floss
That Julie stuck to her knees,

There was soda pop at this little shop
And we ate and drank our fill,
While George went up on a flying fox
And he said: 'Now you be still!'

The evening mist came down at last
And George said we should go,
For Julie Anne was ready for bed
But I said, 'Can't we go?'
I pointed over the other side
Where a stall was draped in black,
With a skeleton painted on the front
Near a man with a bowler hat.

The sign had said 'The Ghost Train'
And it looked all creepy, too,
With little cars that rumbled along
With room on them for two,
So George went over and paid the man
Who gave us an awful leer,
Said, 'Come on kids, here's an empty one,
We can sit you both down here.'

So I sat me down on the outside
Julie Anne was next to me,
The car jerked once, then rumbled off
Through a curtain, I said 'Wheee!'
We travelled into the darkness
With the odd red flashing light,
A spider brushed against Julie's cheek
And she screamed in a sudden fright.

A skeleton stuck out its bony arm
And it made a horrible sound,

Much like the scream of a banshee
Then a monster spun it around,
Its head revolved on its shoulders
And its teeth were yellow and red,
As a witch on a broomstick flew at us
And sailed right over my head.

I think I must have been more than pale
As the train passed ghosts and lights,
And creepy-crawly horror things
That would give you an instant fright,
We went through a darkened spider den
It was then that I looked around,
No Julie Anne, just an empty seat
As the car went thundering down.

I called and called for Julie Anne
But I couldn't hear her scream,
Only the weird and ghostly sounds
As that train passed by in a dream,
But then it parted the curtain and
I found myself in the air,
With George just standing there startled
Running his fingers through his hair.

'What have you done with Julie Anne?'
He shook me, made me sick,
'She disappeared in the tunnel there,
It must be a Ghost Train trick!'
Then George looked round for the barker,
For the man in the bowler hat,
But the man had gone, and the lights went down
And the car sat, still on the track.

'Your mother will kill me,' George had cried
As he dived through the curtain there,
I followed him in, I wouldn't be left
With the crazies at the Fair,
We stumbled over the rails, and fought
The cobwebs and the freaks,
With George still calling out 'Julie Anne!'
In a voice that sounded bleak.

We went right through, saw nobody,
And stood in a sweat outside,
When suddenly there was a rumbling
From a car that was still inside,
The curtain parted, the car came out
With a woman as old as Pan,
She staggered up with a walking stick
And she cried: 'I'm Julie Anne!'

The Music of the Reeds

It had been the worst of years, I seemed
To always be in strife,
First my business in receivership
And then my darling wife,
She decided that our poverty,
Once Banks had seized our home,
Was the perfect opportunity
For her to leave, and roam.

So she roamed with a protector,
The accountant I'd released,
When I found that through his perfidy
I'd have to call the police,

He was always just one step ahead,
My wife knew me too well,
So they took the Channel Ferry, left
This fool, to rot in hell!

I was heading for a breakdown,
All this fretting, and the grief,
I was hell-bent on disaster,
Vowed to catch this blatant thief,
And my wife, I would have killed her
For disloyalty, I swear,
So I followed them through Europe,
Catching glimpses, everywhere.

But they managed to elude me
And I ended up in Greece,
I had gone through all the money
I had salvaged for the chase,
With what little I had left, I found
A villa I could rent,
By a woodland, in the marshes
I could brood on what I'd spent.

It was broken down and basic,
Had been empty there for years,
And the roof was badly leaking,
Rain could mingle with my tears,
I felt sorry for myself, and it
Was lonely, stuck out there,
Where the isolated shepherd came
To see, to stand and stare.

But they soon had lost their interest
In the stranger in their midst,

I was left to brood in silence
Walk the woodland in the mist,
And I skirted round the marshes
Where there lay a shallow lake,
It was fresh, and it was verdant
And unspoiled by man's estate.

When the weather was idyllic
I would sit and think of Beth,
Of the time there on the hillside
Where the world had held its breath,
But the years of wine and flowers
They had slowly been submerged,
And with age, the passion sours
As we lose that primal urge.

I would lie awake at midnight
Hear the music of the reeds,
With the wind so gently playing
Through the marshes and the trees,
And one night I left the villa
When I heard a certain note,
And I saw a sudden movement,
That I thought must be a goat.

But my eyes had slowly focussed,
It seemed old and tired, and turned
And it stared at me quite sadly
It had horns, a beard that curled,
And it stood up on the hindquarters
A goat is noted for,
And it clutched the pipes of Pan
To breathe soft music, from its core.

It stood there for but a moment
Then it walked into the wood,
With its shoulders bowed and beaten,
And it staggered as it moved,
But the music was so wistful
Of a love, long lost before,
That my eyes began to glisten
As the lake lapped at the shore.

In a month I'd met with Gaya
Who I'd seen, back through the trees,
Dancing gently in the moonlight
Casting petals in the breeze,
And she came back to the villa
Where she saw to all my needs,
And we lie in love, and listen
To the Music of the Reeds.

The Awful God

Richard Bryce was a mystery,
He lived on a back street lot,
The house was the old half-timbered sort,
Paint peeled on the old wainscot,
The blinds were drawn through the day and night
And the garden a neighbourhood moan,
Full of the bodies of rusting cars
And creepers, all overgrown.

We rarely saw him out in the street
But he'd peep from the side of blinds,
And stories were told in the neighbourhood
That were often more harsh than kind,

There'd been a wife and a daughter once
But they hadn't been seen in years,
Since the echoing raft of arguments,
Doors slammed, and a flood of tears.

Old Grandpa Bryce had lived in the house
Since thirty odd years before,
He'd worked in the woollen fulling mill
'Til it closed, just after the War,
His son had drowned in the old mill stream,
Was caught in the paddle wheel,
And Grandpa Bryce was left with the child,
To raise, and be brought to heel.

For Grandpa Bryce was a steely man
Who lived his life by the book,
More like a Prophet, this Abraham
Believed, whatever it took,
That 'spare the rod and spoil the child'
Would be how that his Grandson learned,
As he laid the rod across Richard's back
'Til the flesh turned red, and burned.

There was never a ministering angel there
To offer the boy relief,
Only the hard-edged wooden pew
In the church, on a Sunday eve,
And Abraham led the final prayer
In a voice that would damn and blight,
'Beware you sinners, the Awful God
Will come unseen in the night!'

Richard's mother had died in pain
In the blood of the afterbirth,

She never returned to her home again
But was placed, six foot in the earth,
He never knew of a mother's love,
But only a Grandpa's pain,
And Bryce had ruled the daughter and wife
'Til they fled one night, in the rain.

The house was suddenly silent then
Just two of them, left alone,
Grandpa suddenly old and frail,
He never went out on his own,
And Richard boarded the windows up
So you couldn't see in from the street,
It looked like an old abandoned place
'Til the police called round, last week.

We all stood out in the street and watched
As Richard came out of the house,
His hands were cuffed and his hair stood up
And he looked quite down in the mouth,
There must have been twenty cops in there,
All milling around the place,
And one threw up in a paper cup
As we strained to look at his face.

It all came out in a day or two
Just what they had found in there,
The place was sparse, but a giant cross
Stood gaunt in the putrid air,
The skeleton of old Grandpa Bryce
Had been crucified, up tight,
And nailed to his skull: 'The Awful God
Will come unseen in the night!'

Taking Root

I'd seen Lianne at her cottage door
When I'd walked the old bush track,
The cottage had been abandoned, but
She was gradually bringing it back,
She painted it and she patched it
There was nothing she couldn't do,
I even saw her up on the roof
Repairing a faulty flue.

I simply waved at the girl at first
And she'd smile, and wave on back,
She must have been used to seeing me
On that little-used outback track,
I wondered why she would settle there
In a cottage, out on her own,
I never saw anyone else to share
The place that she called her home.

I stopped, of course, and I spoke to her
Once I'd passed a dozen times,
She said that she loved the fresh, clean air,
That she'd travelled from colder climes,
The sun was warm in the early spring
But I mentioned about the drought,
'The summer heat is intense out here
With nothing to keep it out.'

What trees there were had died long since
For the lack of a steady rain,
 They stood, grey, gaunt and twisted, like
Arthritic men, in pain,

She said she was going to grub them out
And plant fresh trees when she could,
Something with lots of leaves for shade
And water them, well and good.

I mentioned a couple of species that
Would grow at a furious pace,
Like the Australian willow, it
Was known for its speed, and grace,
She'd put some in when I passed again
And we talked of family trees,
She said that her Gran had left the place
To her, to do as she pleased.

'My people, back in the early days
Were some of the pioneers,
They built this cottage and tilled the soil
And they persevered for years.
But Gran took off for the city once
Her husband took ill, and died,
He's buried out in the back out there,
With his father, by his side.'

She showed me the graves of her forefathers,
The stones were weathered and worn,
She'd tried to tidy them up a bit
Erected a limestone cairn,
'They came and slaved and suffered here
And died, and followed suit,
That's why I came to save the place,
I felt like taking root.'

I caught a glimpse of her eyes at that
And saw a glimmer of tears,

She was the last of the line of them,
These family pioneers,
She wasn't a striking beauty but
Had passion, guts and grace,
And that's when I fell in love with her
And I told her, to her face.

She smiled and patted my hand: 'You're sweet,
But you don't know me at all,
Maybe you'll get to know me, if
You keep on coming to call.'
So I did, on into the summer then,
And followed through to the fall,
But then I was sent away for months
To a farm where I couldn't call.

She had no phone, she had no mail
No electricity,
She spent her nights on a garden seat
With a lantern on a tree,
The summer had seen a blistering heat
But the fall brought on the rain,
It was well into winter by the time
I was able to call again.

I found her out in the garden, where
She stood in a sort of trance,
I tried to engage her attention, but
She barely spared me a glance,
Her skin was coloured a shade of grey
And her legs were rough and stark,
Her feet had sunk in the mulch out there
And her ankles looked like bark.

I pulled at her hands but she simply leaned,
She swayed like a sapling bent,
Out from the tips of her fingers grew
Some strange disfigurement,
Her hair was tangled with creepers
That were snaking along her back,
I thought I could wake her with a kiss
But I seemed to have lost the knack.

I left her there in the garden, but
I see her from time to time,
The seasons come and the seasons go
But Lianne continues to climb,
Her clothes fell off, they were rotted through
Now she needs no type of suit,
Lianne's as busy as ever,
As she said, she's taking root.

Daydreams

I sit every day in an office, and play
With a ledger that carries my name,
And stare from the window, the clouds scudding grey
On a sky that is always the same,
The river winds down by the weed-winding bank
But is sluggish and slow in its ride,
Heading on out to the estuary, carrying
Debris, adrift on the tide.

Just about here was the place, where in fear
They once straddled the river in chains,
And called up the hundreds, with helmet and shield
To defend this poor land from the Danes,

And often I peer through the rain and the mist
And the grime on the window without,
Imagining Vikings enmeshed in the chains,
And struggling there, to get out.

The office is staffed by grey people in need
Who would like to get home to the wife,
They mutter in tones of their essence and creed
While some of us just want a life,
But Caroline Chambers is not one of these
She's a flower, sprung out of the weeds,
And I see, as she flits between coffees and teas
She's a Saxon, her coffee is mead.

She pushes the trolley that carries the swords
And the helmets, and buckler's too,
As she stands by my desk for a chat and a rest
She's defiant; she's one of the few.
As she stares out the window, I hear her declare
That she's not going to put up with this,
The Danish accountant has stolen her chair
And her venom is mouthed with a hiss.

'I'll poison his coffee, you see if I don't,'
And her Saxon blood comes to the boil,
I get fleeting visions of lopping his head,
Or perhaps we should boil him in oil?
She wanders away and she hands out the pay
As I ravish her there in my mind,
And she stares up at me from a puddle of tea
Mutters, 'How could you be so unkind?'

The following day I can see the affray
As the Legions march into the town,

The Roman Centurions glitter with gold
With their standards held high, not put down,
And Caroline Chambers, Welsh bonnet and dress
With a lilt in her voice, brings the teas,
She stands by the chariot of Boadicea,
Brings the Legions of Rome to their knees!

I sit every day in an office, and play
With a ledger that carries my name,
And stare from the window, the clouds scudding grey
On a sky that is always the same,
But Caroline Chambers has shared in my dreams
Though she has no idea, she's my wife,
As I live in the daydreams of coloured and grey dreams
And desperately search for a life!

The Girl Who Came from the Moon

I noticed the glow through my window-pane,
A glow, set deep in the wood,
I thought that it might be a tree on fire
And it didn't enhance my mood,
I took the jeep, an extinguisher,
And stuck to the well worn trail,
My headlights picked out a wreck of a car
Ablaze, and a girl, quite pale.

Beyond the car was a meteorite
That glowed and pulsed in the dark,
The girl stood shivering, next to a tree
Reached out, and picked at the bark,
She wore a jacket of silver thread
That was scorched, and torn at the seams,

'So this is the place that the Master said,
A planet, cocooned in dreams!'

I thought she was probably quite deranged
And helped her into the jeep,
Her form was slender and angular
And she promptly fell asleep,
I doused the fire in the burning wreck
But the meteorite still glowed,
Buried quite deep in the undergrowth
It was only the top that showed.

I sprayed it all with a burst of foam
But the foam dispersed in the air,
It floated away like candy floss,
The kind you see at the fair,
I turned and made for the Willy's Jeep
And raced back out on the track,
I don't know why, but a shiver ran
From my neck to the small of my back.

Back at the house she looked around
And a smile lit up her face,
'So this is the place you hide at night,
From the monsters, deep in space!'
Her cheekbones were quite angular
And her forehead broad and square,
But the feature most that startled me
Was the sheen of her silver hair.

It fell straight down to her shoulders, swept
Around like a silver bowl,
And looked much more like a helmet, set
For it didn't move at all,

'We'd better see where you're from,' I said,
'Your folks will be worried soon.'
She laughed, a tinkling bell-like sound,
'I just dropped in from the Moon!'

I thought, 'Oh yes, here's a likely one,
Perhaps she should be restrained?'
The shock of the car and the meteorite
Had rendered her quite deranged.
'I came to warn you, the Argonauts
Are waiting, up in the sky,
When Pluto enters Aquarius
They will come, and your race will die!'

I settled her down to sleep the night,
In the morning she was gone,
But out in the woods there were flashing lights
And cars and trucks in a swarm,
There were Police and Special Agents there
And the Army in full force,
While standing silent, watching them there
Was a grey and silver horse.

It watched as a truck had pulled away
With a globe strapped under a tarp,
A bevy of Military Police were there,
By now, it was almost dark,
Then the horse looked back and it stared at me
And I noticed the silver mane,
That swept down over its shoulders
As it cantered off, in the rain.

The Artist's Dilemma

The wind blew in and the wind blew out
And it surged around the eaves,
The door out to the patio slammed
And the yard filled up with leaves,
Then Susan sighed, 'There's goes my ride,
I was going to take the mare,
Now what can we do on a Sunday when
The wind's so wild out there?'

Her aunt lay back on the couch and stared
At me, with her doe-black eyes,
Not much older than Susan, she
Was Venus, in disguise,
Her fingers ran through her coal-black hair
And her hand smoothed down her thigh,
'Why don't you ask the artist, dear,
Before his paints run dry.'

I'd finished painting the background in
Of the leaves that swirled in the air,
But put my palette aside and turned
To look for her meaning there,
Then Susan laughed, as she always did:
'Do you mean that you'd be game?
I've only modelled alone before
But two? It would be insane!'

Imelda slowly uncurled herself
Rose steadily to her feet,
'I'll be the older matron, while
You shall be young, and sweet.'

I shrugged, affecting a nonchalance
That I didn't really care,
But said, 'Okay, I can paint you,
Put your clothes on the old armchair.'

I played about with my palette, mixed
The tones in a kind of blush,
Squeezed the Titanium White, and mixed
It in with the tip of my brush,
And when I finally turned around
They were stood, stark naked there,
I said, 'Clasp hands, then back to back,
And Sue, let down your hair.'

I'd painted my wife a thousand times
So I knew each curve and line,
But Imelda, this was the first I'd seen
And I caught my breath in time,
Her black hair over her shoulders and
Her breasts, so firm and white,
Her hips the marvel of womanhood
And her thighs - a man's delight!

I turned on back to the easel, tried
To steady my shaking hand,
I thought of myself as an artist,
Underneath it, I was a man!
And Imelda caught a glimpse of that
As her lips curled in a smile,
She knew that my heart was pounding,
But my lust would wait for a while.

That painting hangs on the passage wall
And visitors stare in awe,

At the vision of womanly beauty
That the eyes of the artist saw,
And Imelda bridles at compliments
Then gives me the evil eye,
She's often said, there's a place in bed,
But I shake my head, with a sigh!

Rogue Planet

They had promulgated Congress for
The first day of the year,
It would bite into vacations
At the time they most occur,
It would clog the airborne ferries
Overflow the season's trains,
'Whose idea was this, anyway?
You'd think they'd have more brains!'

But the seven thousand members duly
Packed their travel bags,
Posted credit for their spouses,
Sent away their dogs and cats,
For a summons from 'The Lorder'
Was not lightly overlooked,
When he said 'You will attend!' they
Hurried off, their passage booked.

They converged within the Capital
By the Acropolice,
And they filed past the machine guns
In that city known as Neese,
While a rocket called 'Galactic'
Towered high above the dome:

'This begins to look perturbing!'
'Yes - I wish I'd stayed at home!'

Once inside the giant building
That had been a mausoleum,
Now reclaimed at last for government,
Where tombstones still were seen,
The members settled nervously
Each in his numbered seat,
Their sense of pride was tempered
By their memories of defeat.

It was less than fifteen years since their
Corsairs regained the ground
That had been the scene of violence,
Rape and mayhem, all around,
With the citizens assaulted
From their heads down to their feet,
By the battle-weary misfits who
Had ruled each tawdry street.

'We are here to beg the question,'
Said The Lorder, as he stood,
'Do we execute these henchmen,
Do we lock them up for good?
There are thousands in our cellars,
Overflowing all our jails,
Do we risk a massive breakout or
Provide the coffin nails?'

Then a mutter filled the Chamber
From a crowd of bleeding hearts,
They had vetoed execution,
They were men of many parts,

'We may not commend the slaughter
Of so many evil men,
If this Chamber votes for butchery
We'll be as bad as them!'

So the arguments were entered
Back and forth throughout the day,
There would soon be an election
A new Lorder, anyway,
Neither side gained the advantage
The hostility was rife,
Though there was another option,
Banish all of them, for life!

'We can send the ship 'Galactic'
With a thousand at a time,
Take each shipment deep in space
So they will suffer for their crime!
We can drop them on some planet
Where they'll perish from their dearth...'
'Do you know of such a planet?'
'Yes! The Old Rogue Planet, Earth!'

The Fortune Teller

He entered the Fortune Teller's tent
When nobody was around,
He didn't want to be seen in there
By the friends that would put him down,
The woman that sat there, heavily veiled
With her hands on a crystal ball,
Said: 'Cross my palm with silver, sir,
The crystal reveals it all!'

He sat, but nervously sitting there
His mind had become a blank,
All of the questions he'd thought before
Had gone, and his spirits sank.
'I see a lot of confusion here
The crystal echoes your mind,
What was the thing that you wanted most
Of the things that you sought to find?'

He dredged in the recess of his soul,
Just what did he really lack?
His life had been more than successful
There was nothing that he'd take back,
But he felt an awful ache just then
From the pit of his lonely heart,
'I still haven't found a woman to love,
So that will do, for a start!'

She waved her hands on the crystal ball
And he noticed the twisting shapes,
Shadows of past liaisons that
Had passed through his garden gates.

'Perhaps you treat them unfairly
I see tears here by the score,
The women that you rejected, what
On earth were you looking for?'

'I was looking for love,' he stammered out,
He could see she wasn't convinced,
'Love is the one thing left behind
That you haven't revisited since.'
And he thought of June, of Carolyn
And the love that shone from their eyes,
But he'd been so very much younger then
He confessed, and not very wise!

'They were only poor young village girls,
I'd set my heart on a dream,
I wanted a lady of fashion then
A Duchess, even a Queen!'
'Do you think that pearls and coronets
Are the signs of a loving heart?
You'd find the cost of upkeeping them
Are the things that set you apart.'

'There was a girl,' he began again
That I could have loved with my life,'
He stopped and thought about Carolyn,
'I should have made her my wife!'
'I see her, here in the crystal ball
Surrounded by all of your lies,
She loved you once in the wherewithal
But you turned, and cast her aside.'

'Do you think she'd give me a second chance
If I knocked at the girl's front door,

Would she put out the welcome mat for me,
Or wish that I'd never been born?
I must admit I deserve it, I
Have lived my life like a fool,
The dreams I had were beyond me, I
Regret I was ever so cruel!'

'The crystal sees you approach her door,
You're getting down on your knees,
It shows you grovelling on the floor
In a vain attempt to please.'
'I'll do it! She may forgive me then...'
And he left the tent in a spin,
While the Fortune Teller took off her veil
And smiled, did Carolyn!

Hallow Even

Jack found the biggest pumpkin
I had ever seen, I swear,
He wheeled it in a barrow from
The local Pumpkin Fair,
'And what d'you think you'll do with that?'
His sister said, Colleen,
'I'll make a Jack O'Lantern, for
Tonight, it's Halloween!'

'I betcha don't!' 'I bet I do!'
They said, in childish chat,
For Jack was two years older so
He gave her tit for tat,
'I'm gonna dress up like a witch
And put a spell on you,

That thing will end up pumpkin soup
Mixed in my witch's brew!'

'I'll put my clothes on inside out,
Walk backwards round the fire,
My Lantern will bring back the dead,
I'm raising Jim O'Dwyer,
And he will bring the big black sow…'
But that was when she screamed,
His father cuffed him round the head
'Stop frightening Colleen!'

O'Dwyer still hung in chains back then
Had danced his final jig,
He'd strangled little Annie Penn
Then fed her to his pig.
They hung him at the old crossroads
And staked his wicked heart,
And Colleen shut her eyes up tight
When passing, in the cart.

That night they lit the bonfire and
Then went to trick or treat,
The farmers gave them soul cakes
And their wives some home-made sweets,
But Colleen had complained all night
Had moaned and told them lies,
He said, 'You wait 'til we get home,
I'll raise Widow Tresize!'

Tresize had been their schoolmarm
And had caned them as she taught,
Colleen had felt it on her legs
When she and Jack had fought,

The widow ended coughing blood
All over Colleen's dress,
And Colleen screamed as she collapsed,
'Look what you've done - Bad cess!'

She'd always been a spiteful child
And Jack would sit and brood,
Each time his father punished him
For being rough, or crude,
He'd sit up lonely in his room
And tear her dolls apart,
Imagining no sister as
He stuck pins in her heart.

The Lantern sat in pride of place
Out by the great bonfire,
Its evil eyes glowed in the dark,
Its mouth, a dreadful leer,
But Colleen threw a tantrum
Said the face made her feel sick,
She set about it with her broom
And poked it, with a stick.

The pumpkin smashed, in pieces lay
Jack sat with wounded pride,
He took her witches broom and flung it
In the fire, outside,
Another cuff around the head
His anger turned to hate,
And Colleen sniggered just once more
And sealed her morbid fate.

The barrel in the kitchen floated
Apples by the score,

The dunking was the one good thing
That Jack was waiting for,
When Colleen dunked and dunked again
Jack stood behind, and frowned,
Then called out to his father, 'Da!
I think Colleen has drowned!'

The Web

Two old spinsters
Sitting in the barn,
One used candlewick
The other used yarn,
One wore a bonnet
With a white lace trim,
The other bobbed her hair
With a dragonfly pin.

They spun and they spun
'Til the bobbins were full,
They'd squeeze out the knots
Put a twist in the wool,
They spun through the day
And on through the night
And glared at each other
If it didn't look right.

While up in the beams
Of the barn overhead
Two spinsters were spinning out
A gossamer thread,
They stared on down

With their little black eyes
And they spun round the bonnet
And the red dragonfly.

The webs floated down
Were glued to each face
With the spinsters spinning
At a frantic pace.
The wheels stopped spinning
With a sudden click-clack
As the spinsters stared
At those eyes, so black.

As the next day dawned
They came to the barn,
The men and the children
Of that little old farm,
The spinsters were spun
In a giant cobweb,
As they sat, eyes staring -
They were stone cold dead!

Dreamscape

You woke me, crying out in your sleep
That a part of you had died,
I could hear the birds by the window seat
As they woke and chattered outside,
So I turned and shook you gently
Thinking to ease your troubled mind,
'I dreamt I'd been to my wake,' you said,
'And the folk were so unkind!'

'It was only a dream,' I thought to say
But my tongue was swiftly curbed,
You'd slipped so quietly out of the room
And the bed was undisturbed,
I followed, down to the kitchen but
You must have gone outside,
Out by the dear old mulberry bush
I could hear you, as you cried.

Your sister came and she made the tea
You were talking on the phone,
I could hear you in the solarium
So I took my tea alone,
Then I wandered down to the port, to watch
Them load the ships with grain,
And looked for you on the jetty there
But all I could feel was pain.

We've been together for forty years
But something's rearranged,
I think you must be avoiding me
But I love you just the same,

You wave to me from the flower beds
As I sit in the old deckchair,
And read my book in a cosy nook
Then I look, and you're just not there.

You talk to me in my dreams at night
And you say that you love me too,
And we wander hand in hand again
As we always used to do,
But I think that your mind is fading fast
You forget so much today,
But we'll stick together through thick and thin
I'm there for you, come what may.

Your sister summoned the doctor, I
Was out by the kitchen door,
'I think he's looking for you, my dear,
But we'll fool them, like before.'
She said, 'He doesn't accept the fact
That my sister fell asleep,
He'll have to be put in a Nursing Home!'
I sit on the step, and weep!

The Season of the Witch

Most of the country is hushed out there
As the Moon climbs over the hill,
The creatures out in the wild beware
And the air is breathless, still,
The deer is stood at the edge of the wood
Afraid to go in too soon,
With the animals skittish, out in the yard
A hare stares up at the Moon.

There's something amiss in the air tonight
Both furtive and dark, unclean,
Shadows are lurking by old stone walls
In wait for a sign to be seen,
The men all sit in a vacant trance
As the women go out by the ditch,
Wearing their smoke-black cloaks in the dance
For the Season of the Witch.

Then like the flutter of vampire bats
The witches take to their brooms,
Hang on to their tall black pointed hats
And fly low over the tombs,
They head in a swarm up Gallows Hill
Fulfilling some ancient rite,
While watchful eyes at the window-sill
Will get little sleep this night.

For Alison, Lindy, Carmen and Deb
Are watching their mothers leave,
Tucked into bed as their mothers' fled
The girls creep out to deceive,
Pulling the curtains aside they see
The flight go over the hill,
And hear the cackling sounds of glee,
Then the air is cold and still.

Then Lindy calls to the other three
Through the window out to the farm:
'Let's climb up there, where we all can see
What they're doing from high in the barn!'
So they dress themselves in their winter cloaks
And they put on their witches hats

That the mothers had made for Halloween,
Had decorated with bats.

They climbed up over the stacked up hay
To the roof of the timbered barn,
And they peered from the moonlit bullock dray
To the trees by the hilltop farm,
But the witches danced in a grove of trees
Quite hidden from anyone's sight,
'Let's take our brooms,' said Alison Keys
'And fly while the Moon is bright!'

'Let's fly while the Moon is bright,' she said,
So they stood at the edge of the hay,
Looked down to the old paved cattle yard
And the tractor, over the way.
'We saw them fly, we can do it too,
We're witches tonight, we've seen!
Tonight is the magical mystery night
For witches - it's Halloween!'

They mounted their broomsticks, held their breath
Then leapt each one with a scream,
They dropped like stones to the cattle yard
On the night of Halloween,
They were found impaled on the thresher blades
That was parked beside the ditch,
And the screams could be heard a mile away
In the Season of the Witch!

The Guardian of the Pit

He'd worked at the pit since he was ten,
Was quite at home in the dark,
Worked by the light of a miner's lamp
Avoided the slightest spark,
He chipped away at the face of coal,
He chewed tobacco, and spat,
His face was black as he wandered home
With pride in his miner's hat.

But the mine had closed as it petered out
And the miners went on the dole,
While Jack Coltrane had fretted at home
For his work was his very soul,
The entrance tunnels were sealed up tight
And the Colliery wheel was stopped,
It sat like an aging dinosaur
Set high on its wooden props.

The miners drifted away for work
The walls of the houses cracked,
The doors and windows were boarded up
The only one left was Jack,
He wandered lonely about the streets
Of the place he had always known,
The empty terraces, vacant shops
In the town that he'd called his home.

I'd gone to squat in an empty house
I was down on my luck back then,
And Jack had knocked on my nailed up door,
I told him my name was Ben,

He'd pop around for a morning tea
And he'd tell me tales of the mine,
His eyes would gleam with excitement when
He talked of the dust and grime.

'I'll take you there, and show you the pit.'
He knew I'd never been down,
'What else is to do in a place like this,'
He said, and I must have frowned.
'There's nothing to worry about, old son,
Just wrap up well for the cold,
It used to be hot in the workings then,
But we'll be looking for gold.'

He said he knew where the traces were,
He'd seen it a thousand times,
'The owners only wanted the coal
So we left the rest behind,
There's not a lot, but enough for us,
We'll chip out a tidy sum.'
That's all I needed to know, I went
And put some old denims on.

The mine was scary for one like me
Who'd never been down a pit,
So dark and damp, and the air was still,
I hated the smell of it,
We need to go down 300 feet
He said, not batting an eye,
I trudged along in his wake, and thinking:
'Why did I come - Oh why?'

We saw the first few traces of gold
At the thirty fathom mark,

But Jack said, 'Still there's a way to go,'
And he trudged along in the dark,
We walked around the falls from the roof
Where the props had given way,
It was far too late to be turning back
Though I felt a mute dismay.

Suddenly there was a gleam ahead
Lit up by our feeble lamps,
And Jack had hurried ahead to check
What gleamed in the rising damp,
Behind a fall I could see a sight
That will haunt me 'til I'm old,
A skeleton lay in the passageway,
A skeleton covered in gold.

'He must have been here a hundred years,'
Said Jack, 'and there is the proof,
The fall has only revealed him now
The gold has leached from the roof,
It's covered this poor old-timer's bones
He's worth more now that he's dead,'
But then the end of the tunnel glowed
And a voice boomed in my head.

'Who desecrates my dominions,
Who approaches me in their pride?
You come to my underground kingdom
Where another before you died!'
The voice came up through a hole in the ground
That glowed like a fire was lit,
'Retreat, or I'll tear you asunder,
I'm the Guardian of the Pit!'

I don't know how we got out that day
We stumbled and ran to hide,
We thought the demon was at our heels
As we caught at our breath, and cried,
We fell out into the open air
And breathed again at the last,
I said, 'I'll never go down again!'
Jack said, 'It must have been gas!'

'It must have been just a pocket of gas
That we breathed, that knocked us out,
It was just a hallucination
That's for sure,' said Jack, 'No doubt!'
But he never went down the mine again,
He said he was 'over it',
But truth to tell, he was scared as hell
Of the Guardian of the Pit!

The Landau

The winter fogs roll in from the Thames
While frost forms up on the eaves,
The damp will settle in aching bones,
While the trees are bereft of leaves;
The streets were stark in the old East End
A footfall echoed and died,
And nights when the homes were shuttered in
They listened to wheels outside.

A Landau, black as the devil's sin
And drawn by a single horse,
Rolled slowly up to The Black Dog Inn
By the side of the watercourse,

When out there came from the bawdy house
In black from her head to tail,
A dollymop with a nosegay,
Wearing a bonnet, black, with a veil.

She'd climb up into the Landau while
The coachman, clad in a cloak,
Would give one flick with the reins,
And pull on the bit 'til the horse had choked,
He'd take them off with a clatter
Wheels a-rattle on cobblestones,
His eyes agleam like a demon
While he whipped the horse to the bone.

The horse's hooves on the cobbles
Warned ahead through the fog and mist,
As people cowered in doorways
Shouted a curse as the Landau passed,
They followed the glow of the gaslamps
Shedding their weak and feeble light,
And raced by the mighty river
Into the dark of the endless night.

They came to a halt at Wapping
Down where the river cast its spawn,
The bodies of dead and drowned who'd
Cursed their mothers for being born,
And hung on poles at the river's edge
Was another terrible sight,
The bodies of sailor mutineers
That swung in their chains at night.

Hung on the Tyburn gallows
Then cut down and shackled again,

The bodies were coated with tallow
For a post mortem hanging in chain,
They'd bind them up with a winding cloth
Then coat them again in tar,
Hang them in chains at the riverside
'Til their dust blew near and far.

The woman climbed out of the Landau
Took one look, and fell to her knees,
Her lover hung gently swaying,
Swaying in time to the river breeze,
His eyes stared out from the candle wax
And his mouth was shaped in an 'Oh!'
He seemed to be saying, 'Goodbye, my love;
What a terrible way to go!'

She wept like a woman demented,
Seized his legs, and pulled to her breast,
Clung to his swinging figure
Moaned like a creature, quite obsessed,
She tried transferring her warmth to him
But his cold was the cold of death,
And his eyes stared straight ahead of him
No thoughts, no love, no breath!

She climbed back into the Landau
As the coachman whipped it away,
And often at night they hear it go,
Those folks down Wapping way,
They say it spattered a stream of blood
On the road as it raced on by,
From the dollymop who'd slashed her throat
And lay in the coach to die.

And when there's a mighty river fog
In the winter, down by the Thames,
They sit in the Inn they call Black Dog
And they drink to the health of friends,
They drink to the ones who've gone before
As they hear the wheels outside,
And hold their breath at the emptiness
As the door is opened wide!

The Gathering of the Spoils

Marcus Julius rose at dawn,
Splashed water on his face,
He'd spent the night at the Lupanare
With a pretty girl from Thrace,
He saw the glow in the morning sky
But shrugged, and went back inside,
Roused the slave from his slumber
Kicked the dog, sat down and sighed.

She'd cost him three Denarius
And money was getting tight,
The marketplace had been quiet of late
And his purse was rather light,
He'd made just ten Sesterces
With his trade the day before,
People were getting nervous but
He'd seen it all before.

Whenever the ground was trembling
As it often used to do,
They thought of the massive earthquake
That had hit in '62,

It had razed the Apollo Temple,
They were still rebuilding now,
Seventeen years of minor quakes
Had slowed the work right down.

But life went on, and food was dear
With slaves not worth their keep,
He only had one, Antonius,
And all that he did was sleep,
It might have been easier with a wife
So Marcus thought aloud,
But out in the street, he heard the feet
And the cries of a nervous crowd.

The sky had suddenly darkened
So they fled, the feeble hearts,
Blocking the ancient carriageway
With their chariots and carts,
He watched the crowd from his window
The Plebeians hurried past,
Soldiers and patricians all
In a jostling, shouting mass.

The slave of Marcus Julius
Was more than terrified,
So he chained him fast to an iron ring
By the strongroom, deep inside,
'It's only a passing wonder,
We're not going anywhere!'
He locked his door to the street,
Stood by the window space, and stared.

He noted the noble families
Go struggling past his door,

Carrying all of their wealth with them,
And the women carried more,
The day grew dark as a midden
'Til you couldn't see ahead,
And people screamed for each other
As the younger ones had fled.

Eleven o'clock, it settled down
He ventured into the street,
Lying in piles were goods they'd dropped
In the jostling, and the heat,
For the temperature was rising fast
As he seized what he could find,
Cases of ladies jewellery,
And purses they'd left behind.

He piled the goods in the strongroom
Then got ready to shelter there,
Brushed off the pyroclastic ash
That had settled in his hair,
He laughed out loud as he closed the door
But paused by the slave to say:
'Our lives are going to get better, I'm
The richest man in Pompeii!'

Courting Disaster

I was twenty-three when I saw her first,
Without a word of a lie,
She had wandered into the woods by me
With a basket, held on high,
Her auburn hair reflected the sun
And she flashed me a dazzling smile,

That turned my head to the way she led
As I followed her, over the stile.

She skipped along at a steady pace
Weaved in and out through the trees,
Collected the broad-rimmed mushrooms there
As she stopped, and fell to her knees,
Her dress flared out as it caught the wind
And her hair was floated wide,
I hid by a tree, and held my breath
As I thought of her, as a bride.

She had such a look of innocence,
Was free as the birds of the air,
The legs and the grace of a peasant girl
Brought up in the great out-there,
She ran right up to a Woodsman's house
That was hidden by branch and vine,
Then danced right in through the open door,
And then I knew; she was mine!

The door was closed when I finally knocked
But I heard a terrible moan,
And minutes later the door unlocked,
In the hall stood a fusty crone,
She stared at me through her hoary eyes
With never a hint of grace,
'What do you want?' she growled at me,
For the shock must have shown in my face.

'That girl, who danced in a moment back,
I'm here to discover her name.'
'There is no girl,' said the ancient hack,
'You'd better return where you came!'

'I saw her enter, I must insist,
I'll not be gulled by your lies!'
'That girl's been dead for a long time back,
You'd better leave now, if you're wise!'

She slammed the door in my face just then
So I wandered back through the trees,
A raincloud covered the midday sun
And I felt the chill of a breeze,
The rain came down as I walked back home,
Climbed over the ricketty stile,
Was drenched to the skin as I wandered in,
And thought to resort to guile.

For days I lingered by that old track,
The place that I'd seen her first,
I felt so miserable, holding back,
As I thought, and feared for the worst,
What if the girl was a sprite, who'd died,
Just as the old crone said?
Try as I might, I couldn't believe,
Nor get her out of my head.

I finally went to the Woodsman's house
And I hid in a patch by the vine,
When suddenly out of the door came tripping
The girl, with her eyes a-shine,
She skipped away with her basket, filled
With linen and loaves and cheese,
And I caught her then in a shady glade
As she stopped, and fell to her knees.

'I hoped you'd come,' were the words she said
As she laid a cloth on the ground,

'I have to hide from that grey old witch
So I go where I'll never be found.'
She broke the bread and she poured the wine
And we ate and drank in the glade,
My mind was filled with a sudden chill
But I thought of fun in the shade.

'So when are you going to kiss me, then?'
She said when we finished our feast,
'I've fed your animal spirits, now,
It's time I was paid, at least!'
I kissed her there in the shady glade
And we tumbled there in the leaves,
Then I fell asleep, and she'd gone when I
Awoke, and the heart, it grieves.

I stumbled home, but was feeling faint
I had aches and pains in my head,
I staggered through to the bedroom, then
I found her asleep in my bed,
She woke and sat, and she stared at me
But her face had begun to change,
There were lines and wrinkles around her eyes
And her hair was grey with age.

'I need you now that my time is short,
Come and rest your weary head,'
I caught a glimpse in the mirror then
And it filled me full of dread,
For the face of a man of middle age
Stared back at me from the glass,
'Just what have to done to me?' I said…
'Do you really have to ask?'

'I fed on your animal needs, and you
Gave something to set me free,
If you want me to be a bright young thing
Then you must replenish me.'
I saw she aged by the minute there
And she soon let out a moan,
For lying in bed was a figure of dread,
That hoary old witch, the crone!

I'm far too weak to get out of bed,
But Elli goes out on her own,
She carries her basket into the wood
For the mushrooms she eats alone,
My beard is grey and I dread each day
As she bleeds my life from its core,
But she's as lovely as ever she was
At a hundred and twenty-four!

Vanishing Point

I'd noticed the girl a dozen times
As she passed me on the street,
All I could see were those red-rimmed eyes
And that look of pure defeat,
So often I thought to stop her there
To ask her what was wrong,
But I lived in a part of the city where
Such weakness didn't belong.

We all sit huddled in high rise flats
And keep ourselves to ourselves,
We don't get involved with the neighbours,
Heaven forbid that we should be friends,

We eye each other suspiciously
On the dark and dingy street,
And try to walk in the shadows
So that our passing will be discreet.

But often I'd pass the local cop
As he put the posters up,
'Does anyone know the whereabouts…'
But nobody even stopped,
So many faces on poles and posts
And the names they would annoint,
Of those who'd gone to the edge of the world,
Right through to the Vanishing Point!

I often wondered about them all,
Was it easier to escape?
Was life such a terrible martyrdom
In the hands of a fickle fate?
So many were lost with every year
Was it murder, mayhem or less,
How many husbands misplaced their wives
In an act of carelessness?

The girl intrigued me, every day
She would pass by the corner shop,
But I never saw her happy or gay
She'd the weight of the world on top,
She slowly became insubstantial, like
A wraith that was taking the air,
I followed her round from a distance
Watched her enter the Pearly Fair.

There were clowns and strange hobgoblins there,
And often a Harlequin,

They wandered around in a daze, it seemed
Like a circus about to begin,
And not one had an identity
Apart from the paint they wore,
A slight disguise in a world of lies
Said, 'What did we come here for?'

The girl got changed for the Judy Show
Full size, and Punch was a man,
He beat her there with a wooden club
As the audience clapped their hands,
The 'club' was really a cardboard roll
But it must have hurt like sin,
And Judy cried as the audience died,
'I'm back in the world again!'

I followed her down to the waterside
At dusk, with its evil smell,
And others, still in their sad disguise
Were milling around, as well,
They warmed themselves by a brazier
And looked for a place to sleep,
But 'Judy' stood by the empty dock
And the water there was deep.

My eyes played tricks in the dimming light
She started to fade away,
Became as one with the falling night
Where the lost and the beaten pray,
She was there one minute and gone the next
The movement was so adroit,
The water formed like a giant tear
Right there, at the Vanishing Point!

Karma

He looked down over the valley,
Over the verdant green and trees,
And suddenly felt so humbled
That he sighed, and fell to his knees,
He'd only been out a single day
With the world before him spread,
So still he could hear those prison gates
As they'd clanged behind, in his head.

He'd finished his twenty seven years
He'd paid society's due,
Locked in a cell of eight by ten
For the things that he'd had to do,
He'd shown no mercy to Annabel,
No more to the Widow Peak,
He'd drowned them, just as he meant to do
When they'd met, in less than a week.

He thrilled at the thought of their staring eyes
As he held them down in the bath,
Watching their lives leach out of them,
Just as he'd done with Kath,
There'd been so many, he'd not confessed
But been convicted for two,
The other ten would have got him life
Without reprieve, if they knew.

He went to live in the valley
Rented a cottage under the trees,
Owned by a man called Anderson
Who'd visited him for years,

He'd said he knew of a valley where
He could start his life again,
He'd said, 'Now here is your second chance,
Back in the world of men!'

He wandered round in the cottage
Took in the bathroom at a glance,
Took in the nice deep marble tub
With a smirk and a rub of his hands,
The village was just a walk away
But he'd give it a day or two,
Then check for a widow or single girl
At the store, as he wandered through.

He spent the night reminiscing
Thinking of all those staring eyes,
Of Kristen Poole, that silly young fool
That he'd fed with outrageous lies,
Her mouth had flapped like a goldfish
As she fought in a bleak despair,
But nearly a foot of water lay
Between her face and the air.

And who was that girl, that Marigold,
That he'd met in the Shop 'n Save?
He'd thought that her name was Sanderson,
She didn't know how to behave,
She'd said her brother looked out for her
Would interfere with her fun,
But once in a bath of water,
It would only be fun for one.

He lay and stared at the ceiling as
He felt quite suddenly cold,

The name of his mentor Anderson
Came creeping back to his soul,
He heard the rushing of water
Off in the distance, up on the heights,
And made his way to the village
Lying in darkness, deep in the night,

The cottages all were empty
So was the chapel, totally bare,
The door of the shop was open
Nothing but garbage left in there,
He turned and ran up the village street
But the thunder was hard at his heels,
When a wall of water, ten feet high
Rushed over the verdant fields.

They'd opened the sluices at the dam
To flood the Valley at night,
To turn it into a reservoir
For a city that lay nearby,
The villagers had been gone for a month
But they stood and they watched the tide,
Flooding their tiny cottages
While Anderson laughed, and cried!

Fair Exchange

Two soldiers sat in the rubble
Out by the Berlin autobahn,
Schulz had once been an artist, while
Ludwig came from a farm,
They huddled down as the allied planes
Roared over, dropping their bombs,
The war was pretty well done with,
They were going back to their homes.

Their Units long had been shattered
As they retreated over the Seine,
While Hitler raved in his bunker
That they should hold out, just the same,
They knew their lives would be forfeit
If they were seen there, out in the street,
So only moved in the darkness,
Prayed for the peace that came with defeat.

They each of them carried a shoulder pack
Of things they were taking back,
Some bread, a twist of tobacco
Something to barter for Cognac,
Ludwig's pack seemed to wriggle about,
To Schulz it was awful big,
And so, to allay curiosity,
He told Schulz, it was a pig!

'I'll need it back on the farm,
Something to breed from in the peace,
The army took all our livestock,
And the farm is still on a lease.

My wife is probably starving
And the kids won't know me at all,
I found it in a deserted farm
And I plucked it over a wall.'

'And what have you got in *your* pack,'
Ludwig asked, 'a chicken or two?'
'Or maybe a slice of bratwurst,
Give me a look, I'm hungry too!'
'Nothing that you could eat,' said Schulz,
'I've a painting by Matisse,
Part of the plunder of Goering,
Fell off a truck that was heading east.'

The ground was shaking with falling bombs,
They had to cover their ears,
'I've had enough of this war,' said Schulz,
His eyes were filling with tears,
Then out of the firestorm came a man
Stumbling through the gap,
With an SS badge at his collar
And a Death's Head badge on his cap.

He pulled out his Luger, covered them,
And sneered at the uniform,
'Another couple of cowards, eh?
You'll wish you'd never been born!
The Fuhrer says I should shoot you now,
So tell me, why should you live?'
'The war is done, if you let us run,
We may have something to give.'

So Ludwig opened his pack a shade
And showed the soldier his pig,

'You can have yourself a mighty roast,
You won't find another as big.'
'And you, what prize can *you* offer me?'
'I've got a real Matisse...'
'I'll take it all,' said the SS man,
'It'll sit on my mantelpiece!'

He took the packs and he backed on out
Went stumbling out in the blitz,
When suddenly there was an awful blast
And the man was blown to bits.
'The pig must have wriggled and pulled the pin
Of the hand grenade in the pack;
We can thank the gods, or providence,
That could have been me in the hat!'

The SS cap was covered in blood
Had landed at Ludwig's feet,
He grinned at Schulz, said: 'Fancy that!
I hope you can be discreet.'
'There goes a priceless Matisse,' said Schulz,
'But fair exchange, if we live,
I'm sorry about your porker, but
There are several types of pig!'

The Stalker

She looked demure as she came on board
And sat in a corner seat,
And Paul looked up from his paper as
She crossed her legs in the heat,
The blouse she wore had a bunch of lace,
Her skirt rose over the knee,
And a length of thigh had caught his eye
As the train had gathered speed.

'Some girls were there for the taking,'
Paul had thought, and he shook his head,
They weren't alive to the dangers that
Their wiser mothers would dread,
So many girls were assaulted
On the track that led to the train,
They needed a good Samaritan;
Outside, it started to rain.

A man came into the carriage
Sat across on the other aisle,
He tried to catch her attention with
Some twisted sort of a smile,
He made a pointed remark, at which
She scowled, but made no reply,
But Paul sat watching and listening
To the man with the evil eye.

The girl stood up as the train pulled in
To the village of Little Cross,
And the man got ready to leave the train
But waited, 'til she'd got off,

131

So Paul jumped up on a whim, and thought
To follow, and keep her safe,
He'd keep his eye on this other guy
Be there for her, just in case.

The track led over some common land
Then wandered into a wood,
The girl ploughed on, didn't look back
Though Paul had thought that she should,
The man took off on a side track then
And soon was lost to his view,
Where the ground was covered with thickets
Sparkling still with the morning dew.

The girl had vanished ahead of him
Round a bend in the beaten track,
Paul was hurrying after her
When he heard a sound at his back,
He turned and he saw the girl approach
And knew that he was in strife,
For glittering in her hand he saw
The long curved blade of a knife.

She stabbed him once, she stabbed him twice
She stabbed him a dozen times,
She snarled, 'Is this what you wanted, No?
Well isn't that a surprise!'
He toppled back as she scythed at him
And tried to catch at his breath,
The words, 'I thought to protect you,'
Left unsaid, in the throes of death.

They took his wallet, they took his ring
As his blue eyes glazed at the sky,

'He thought that I was the stalker,' grinned
The man with the evil eye,
She turned to him an excited smile
And murmured, 'Gee, that was fun!
Let's take the train to the Junction, Joe,
And get us another one!'

The Wood of Forgotten Deeds

I'd been depressed for a year or so
For the way ahead was grim,
Each venture failed left a legacy
That had said, 'You can't come in!
No smell of sweet success for you
But the canker of despair.
Don't hope for wealth or accolades
In your life, they're just not there.'

My wife took off with a businessman
That I once had called a friend,
I hadn't known what was going on
'Til she left me, in the end,
The lure of money and trinkets turned
Her face from a dismal past,
And her one delight was to scorn me then
When her love failed, at the last.

I often thought that I'd end it then
When my world was black as pitch,
When the future promised more of the same
In some unforgiving ditch,
I wondered why it had chosen me
This fate, with its barren seeds,

But came at last to the truth, I found
The Wood of Forgotten Deeds.

I'd travelled far from the paths of men
To nurse my hurts on my own,
Squatted in many a ruined house
And wandered at night, alone,
I came at length to a valley where
No man had laid his hand,
And a wood had covered the valley floor
Since the dawn of time began.

Rain had driven me into the wood
To shelter among the trees,
And a mood of some despair had grown
As it forced me to my knees,
My mind lit up with a thousand things
That littered my wayward past,
And every tree cried out to me:
'Each sin is nailed to your mast!'

The things that I was ashamed of
I had pushed them away from me,
Hidden them in my subconscious so
They wouldn't keep bothering me,
But in this wood was a memory
Of everything mean and grim,
The things I'd tried to forget were there
And forced me to take them in.

The petty slights and injustices
That I'd scattered, far and wide,
The friends that I'd turned my back on
When it was just a question of pride,

I'd never thought of the consequence
For them, or who I had hurt,
But blithely left in my ignorance
The ones I'd left in the dirt.

And then I came to a vision
That had haunted me, on and off,
A girl that had gone to prison
I could have saved if I'd cared enough,
I'd left her pregnant and wanting there
So she'd stolen food for the child,
The magistrate said, 'Fifteen months!'
The thing that I'd done was vile.

A fit of remorse came over me
And I wept and wailed in the wood,
My fate was suddenly clear to me
I'd only got what I should!
I'd never bothered to see the child
Or see to its tender needs,
But thanked the spirit that came to me
In the Wood of Forgotten Deeds.

I travelled back and I found the girl
And I begged for a second chance,
She said she had nothing but hate for me
But we finally found romance,
My life came out of that darker place,
I see to all of their needs,
She's my Sun, my Moon and Stars, I thank
The Wood of Forgotten Deeds!

Mistaken Identity

The mother lay in a stupor filled
With alcohol and drugs,
The twins lay wet in the carry-cot
And screamed at the top of their lungs,
The boyfriend of the moment sat
At a bar in a nearby town,
Drinking away the welfare cheque
And taking them further down.

Sally Pearce was a homely girl
As such, and easily led,
Many a teenage male had found
His way to her maiden bed,
They bought her favours with alcohol
And hooked her on cocaine,
They so befuddled her mind that she
Could not remember her name.

So Jack had her in the morning when
The sun was low in the sky,
While Derek had her at lunch when she
Had snorted coke, and was high,
She carried the seeds of both of them
And both of them found a home,
Embedded deep in her ovaries
As she lay drugged out, alone.

So when she heard she was having twins
She didn't know who to blame,
But thought it must be the first of them
So gave the twins Jack's name,

She didn't know that their fathers were
As different as chalk and cheese,
For Jack passed on a criminal gene
While Derek passed S.T.D's.

The first one born was Timothy,
With a mop of jet black hair,
Then twenty minutes to follow on
Came Adam, so pale and fair,
They could have been Cain and Abel
If she'd only studied the book,
For Adam was such a happy child
While Tim had an evil look.

She hardly saw them growing up
They learned to fend for themselves,
They'd go and ransack the kitchen
Pulling the food right off the shelves,
The boyfriends came and the boyfriends went
In a long, continuous line,
They didn't know what a father was
Nor a mother, most of the time.

The only love that they ever knew
Was their love for the brother twin,
For they were the only constants as
The others came out and in,
While Adam took to his books and proved
A whiz at Math in his school,
Timothy fought a constant war
To tell the truth, he was cruel.

He punched the boys and tortured the girls
And dipped their plaits in the ink,

Protected Adam from bullies and fools
But never had cause to think,
Adam went on to Uni while
Timothy took to the street,
Dealing in drugs, and taking home
Enough for his mother to eat.

Adam had met a girl called Gaye
She liked that his eyes were brown,
He gave her his sophomore ring one day
Escorted her round the town,
She wanted to meet his brother, Tim
But Adam would not be drawn,
He said that his brother had gone away
'Til he called one day, to the dorm.

Timothy's eyes had met with Gaye's
And they felt a shock of delight,
For opposites often attract, they say,
As day will follow on night,
For Gaye was ripe with an innocence
That will fall for an evil spell,
So Timothy started meeting her
In the quad, by the old stairwell.

They found her body at Easter-time
Down an old storm-water drain,
Raped and beaten, her throat was cut,
And they said, 'He must be insane!'
Adam was taken down to the cells
And grilled for almost a day,
'You were the girl's last boyfriend,
We'll be taking your D.N.A.'

The D.N.A. was almost a match
Enough for a guilty plea,
While Adam strongly denied the charge,
'It certainly wasn't me!'
He didn't mention his brother's name,
But hoped he would see the day
When Timothy came to visit him,
But Timothy went away.

They came for him in the dawning light
And marched him into the shed,
His lips were trembling as he stood
And bit his lip 'til it bled,
'Any last words you'd like to say
Before you pay for your sin?'
The rope had tightened around his neck
When he almost whispered, '…'

The Passing

The change, it comes so slowly
Like the winter of our lives,
It encroaches while we're playing,
While we're laughing with our wives,
As the children wave goodbye
The first brief chill will still the air,
And that silence settles on us
As they turn, and close the door.

Then we stare long at each other
But we find no words to say,
You have been the faithful mother
That I married, back some way,

But I see your smile has faded
With the passing of the years,
And you turn your face away so I
Won't see that trace of tears.

Are you thinking of that moment
When you held that new born child,
Of the joy of those first steps, or of
The day your baby smiled?
And the schooling and the learning
And the knees they brought home skinned,
Or the pride you took each time you watched
That graduation film.

While I find my own thoughts turning
To those days before we wed,
To your awesome, breathless beauty
As you passed, and turned my head,
Of that first-time kiss I savoured
Out beneath the apple tree,
When I took you to my heart, and you
First said you wanted me.

Now we're grey, and more like shadows
Since the lust in us has died,
And we rarely touch each other
Since we turned to ash inside,
For the years of work and struggle
Took their toll on you and I,
And I hear you every evening as
You go outside to cry.

All those dreams that ended shattered,
All those hopes that turned to tears,

Here we sit, both disillusioned
With the tolling of the years,
And we pass our friends unseeing
As we wander in the street,
We are ghosts, a long time passing
Now our story is complete.

We are like the leaves of autumn
That have fallen from the trees,
Blowing through our days unspoken
With each passing, gentle breeze,
We will fade and be forgotten
In the long term way of things,
But we'll cling in desperation for
What each last moment brings.

The Inn of Jasper Shrine

The coast was rugged and storm-swept as
I battled it in the rain,
The cliffs reared up, then fell away
To a flat, deserted plain,
The sea beat up in a thunder on
The rocks that lined the shore,
When I saw the wreck of a wayside inn
And its open, swinging door.

It hadn't appeared on the map, I knew
As I'd studied the bleak terrain,
The thing that I'd come here looking for
Was a wreck from the Spanish Main,
It lay in fifteen fathoms there
With a load of gold moidores,

141

Chased inshore by a privateer
And sunk, so my uncle swore.

He'd come on some ancient manuscripts
And the log of the Brig 'Despair',
Washed up a hundred years ago
On the coastline near Llan Fair,
It roamed the seas three hundred years
Without a crew or a sail,
The log said most of the crew were dead
Tipped out by a great white whale.

The bones of the Captain, Peverell,
Lay slumped, right over the log,
It told of the Spanish galleon
And where it went down in the fog,
It told how the whale had tipped the brig
And broken the mast in two,
While the rest of the men had died of thirst
As it drifted, with the crew.

I came to the shelter of the Inn
And could read the swinging sign,
It carried a skull and a bottle of rum
And a name, 'The Jasper Shrine',
The door hung loose on its hinges and
Gave out a creak and a moan,
The wind howled in at the windows
As the timbers swayed and groaned.

The storm continued to rage outside
At least I was warm and dry,
I lay that night on the upper floor
And stared straight up at the sky,

The thatch had fallen in holes and rain
Came pouring down in a stream,
But I was tucked in a corner, dry,
And there I began to dream.

It must have been two o'clock or so
When I heard a ghostly tap,
Of someone shuffling with a crutch
Then a mighty thunderclap,
A lantern gave out a ghastly light
Threw shadows along the stair,
And then a woman, her voice rang out,
'Oh what, and who is it there?'

I peered on down and could see the wench
Her bonnet trimmed with lace,
But the burly sailor standing there,
I couldn't quite see his face,
Their dress was that of another time
When pirates sailed the sea,
The sailor brought down his cane with a crash,
'They call me Cap'n Teague.'

'Some pottage girl, and a brace of rum
To warm this sailor's cheeks,
My ship's aground and my fate's undone
I'm stranded here for weeks!'
'You'll need to show me the King's good coin
Before you bite or sup,
I've had you sailors before round here
And you're hard on paying up.'

'I have a chest of dubloons,' he said
Moidores, and Spanish lace,

My chest will be here in the morning, girl,
So lift your pretty face,
Shift and get me the vittals that
Will warm my aching bones…'
'No rum, not even a little,'
Said the girl, and turned to go.

Teague had bellowed and crashed his cane
Across the wench's head,
She fell at the foot of the stairs, and groaned
As her bonnet turned blood red,
'I'll serve myself you foolish wench
Do you dare to challenge me?'
But the girl had stirred, rolled over
And cried out, 'By God, you'll see!'

She pulled from out the folds of her dress
An ancient matchlock gun,
Cocked the trigger then aimed and fired
As the Captain turned and spun,
He hit the floor with a cry of pain
And the lantern flew out wide,
The light went out, and all I could hear
Was the sound of the turning tide.

I hid for the rest of the night, afraid
To venture down the stair,
I was cautious still in the morning
Thinking I'd find them dead down there,
But nothing lay in the dawning light
But the sign of time's contempt,
The floor was littered in seaweed and
Some old rat excrement.

My friend came up in a trawler
As we'd planned in the weeks before,
I'd quit the Inn for the final time
Took off through the swinging door,
We never came on the Spanish ship
But the Inn played on my mind,
I wondered, was it a dream or a ghost
At the Inn of Jasper Shrine?

Peter Pan

He'd buried his head in manuscripts
And books for twenty years,
He'd kept himself to himself had never
Ventured down the stairs,
His meals were brought on a silver tray
His clothes were laundered and pressed,
No callers came to his stately rooms
To invade his hours of rest.

He'd turned his back on the world out there
When young, and his sister went,
His parents left the estate to him
Though most of the money was spent,
He had no interest in state affairs,
No more in the works of man,
Looked rarely out of the windows
Of his mansion, Maison Grande.

He studied the force of nature,
Tempests, storms, tornado files,
Read books on the brontosaurus,
Mammoths, raptors, crocodiles,

The only women he knew of,
Little girls like his sister Ann,
He lived like a boy forever
In his mind, like Peter Pan.

He didn't hear when the Bailiffs
Took his furniture from below,
Cleaned out the candelabra
Caused his silver trays to go,
Ripped up the hallway carpet
Took the Louis the XVI chairs,
And finally came up knocking
When they exhausted the loot downstairs.

He stood in shock when they carried off
His desk of Baltic Pine,
Ripped the books from the shelves and
Took the last of his stock of wine,
He saw the bills he'd neglected when
The cook came up to quit,
Her owed her three months wages and
That was the least of it.

The man from the real estate came up,
A man called Arty Hook,
The name sat deep in his memory
Had he read it in some old book?
The Maison Grande would have to be sold
Could he please vacate it now,
The outside world burst into his head
Ran furrows across his brow.

His sister came to lead him away,
He went confused, like a child,

He didn't know what he'd have to do
But his thoughts were running wild,
There were people here, and people there
Each wanting a piece of him,
But he had nothing to offer them,
The future was looking grim.

Ann had a friend called Wendy who
Came round to see to his needs,
The first real woman he'd seen up close
Since before his early teens,
He noticed the perfume that she wore,
And watched her walk with a sway,
The child that had lived in the Maison Grande
Was slowly drifting away.

He felt her breath caressing his cheek
When she leaned in close to speak,
And sensed the draw of those ruby lips
And the softness of her cheek,
Her body warmth seemed to comfort him
When they sat on the old divan,
'Til the night she said, in her negligée,
'It's time to make you a man!'

They called around to the real estate
Next day, and collared Hook,
'We won't be selling the Maison Grande
You can take it off your book.
For Wendy's paid off the debtors, and
We're planning to move back in,
I remember you, and the crocodile,
You can try but you'll never win!'

He got a job at the Uni with
The knowledge he had in store,
And made his mark as a tutor
Teaching English Literature,
While Wendy used all her talents to
Remodel the Maison Grande,
And he excelled with his students
When he was teaching Peter Pan.

The Fair Weather Man

There are times when fate steps in, and then
You never stand a chance,
For your life is cut and tailored to
Some random fortune's dance,
So it was with Esmerelda
Who I'd loved with all my life,
And if fortune had but favoured me
She would have been my wife.

We'd long been courting, on and off
Before the seventh grade,
I had planned our lives minutely
Roads set out, and footpaths paved,
She always seemed to go along
With every scheme I'd planned,
'Til the one thing I'd not factored in
Appeared, his name was Stan!

He came in a Ferrari like
Some flashy movie star,
In his blazer, hat and silk cravat,
She gazed long at his car,

In a moment then, of weakness
She went with him for a drive,
And returned, my Esmerelda with
His star bright in her eyes.

It was Stan is this, and Stan is that
And Stan, can do no wrong,
She went with him Bungee Jumping,
Took to wearing a sarong,
And while I would cling to steeples, cleaning,
Painting, like King Kong,
He was with her, titillating,
Though I'd told her, it was wrong.

She began to sulk, took off the ring
And flung it in my face,
So I ground it into powder
(I admit, the ring was paste);
But she never did come back to me
Was more than mesmerised
By this flashy interloper who'd
Infiltrated our lives.

Then Stan went parachuting
Jumped from 20,000 feet,
He could land right on a nickel
In the middle of a street,
(So he said), but no-one questioned,
Esmerelda less than most,
He was more than her Prince Charming,
He'd become the perfect host.

I should have known the cause was lost,
I should have dried my eyes,

When folk spoke of their wedding
It still caught me by surprise,
They'd planned it for St. Albans
In that ancient little church,
With the tallest, sharpest steeple
In the county, and that hurt.

Their choice was quite ironic
I had been aloft that spire,
To clean a hundred years of grime
A steeple will acquire,
I'd cleaned up to the pinnacle,
Down to the bell-house tower,
And felt that little church was mine,
My mood was more than dour!

But Stan was not content to walk
The aisle, to greet his bride,
He planned to parachute on down
To the courtyard, just outside,
Where Esmerelda, dressed in white
Would gaze up at the skies,
To watch him come from up above
The lovelight in her eyes.

The day was wet and blustery,
The weathercock spun round,
The tiny plane flew overhead
Stan leapt toward the ground,
He looped, side-slipped, and swooped and turned
Put on a great display,
The daring groom would seem to zoom
From heaven, to earth's soft clay.

The guests stood in the courtyard, raised
Their eyes up to the sky,
As Stan approached, I saw the tears
In Esmerelda's eye,
But then a sudden, wayward gust
Spun Stan too far around,
And skewered him on the steeple
Fifty yards above the ground.

I hesitate, but mention now
How blood flew from his mouth,
Shot over Esmy's wedding dress
Its stream still flowing south,
He draped there like an old rag doll
He twitched, and kicked, and hung,
I think they called the wedding off
Before the day was done.

They turned to me, the Steeplejack,
And said, 'Well, it's like this,
We'll need to get the steeple cleaned,
Unskewer the detritus…'
I looked the Pastor in the eye
And said, 'From where I stand,
He's yours and Esmerelda's now,
Your own Fair Weather Man!'

End of a Rat

He walked the length of the village street
With a board - 'The End is Nigh!'
In a dirty army overcoat,
He looked like a nice old guy,
But kids would jeer as he drank his beer
From a bottle outside the pub,
In winter, fend off the snowballs
That they threw - aye, there's the rub!

For he had served with the Desert Rats
When the Aussie's held Tobruk,
Had gone out under a blazing sun
Where an egg on the sand would cook,
He'd taken three light German tanks
With his mates from the Aussie bush,
On a night patrol where they had to crawl
Then fight like the Sydney Push.

After the war, he'd met a girl
In Alexandria,
One of the W.A.A.C.'s that served out there,
Her name was Angela,
He followed her back to England where
She turned her badges in,
And married the girl in Leicestershire,
But never went home again.

They settled down in a village there
Though he yearned for sand and sun,
She said she'd never leave England while
Her life had time to run,

He found some work on a local farm
Though he often became depressed,
And thought of the beach at Bondi and
The wheat fields of the west.

They lived and loved for forty years
Though he felt quite beaten down,
The locals never accepted him
As a native of the town,
His wife took sick to her bed one day
And said, 'the time has come,
You'd better go back to Australia now
That my life is nearly done.'

She died as the sun was coming up
On the bleak, flat Leicester plain,
He buried her there in a cemetery
With an Anglo-Saxon name,
He thought to leave but her spirit stirred
And he couldn't leave her grave,
But went to the age-old Norman church,
Knelt in the nave, and prayed.

For years he studied the Bible there
Considering all he'd done,
The bones of the soldiers left out there
In the terrible Libyan sun,
The emptiness of his life took hold
And he walked with a weary sigh,
Placing a board around his neck
That said - 'The End is Nigh!'

He walked with his head bowed down and low
And forgot to turn around,

They found him frozen, covered in snow
Just a mile outside the town,
A photograph of his wife was tucked
In the band of his old slouch hat,
And on his lapel, a medal cast
In the shape of a Desert Rat!

Lost Girl

My girl went out on a Saturday night
They said that she was alone,
I'd said, 'We'll meet at the Cineplex,'
But the movie was postponed,
I waited there in the vestibule
For an hour, or maybe more,
But she made me feel a total fool
And I left by the same front door.

Where are you Ruth, now tell me the truth
Did you go to meet some guy,
Did you think the movie a total bore,
Did you plan to go and get high?
Your friends all said you're a scatterbrain
And I think they might be right,
But you've been gone for a couple of days
And your mother's taken fright.

She called the cops when I went around
To see what happened to you,
Your mother thought we had spent the night
So she had a piece of me too,
I told her I hadn't seen you, girl
Since the Friday afternoon,

Her face went white, and her eyes were bright
With the tears that she cried for you.

So where have you gone, my Ruth, my girl
Since you wandered into the town,
Did you walk right past the Cineplex
And carry on further down,
Where the lights are bright in the dead of night
And the clubs begin to rage,
With the music's beat in the summer heat,
Did you walk right off my page?

They called me in and they grilled me there
At Precinct Forty Six,
A squad of detectives yelled at me
'Til I thought they were having fits.
I told them you hadn't met me there
But they said that it was a lie,
I couldn't answer their questions
Cross my fingers, and hope to die!

A lawyer came in to see me
So they had to let me go,
And now I wander about the streets
Just looking for you, you know.
I tried to phone but they found your cell
In some old back alley bin,
Behind the Hospital Organ Store
But they wouldn't let me in.

I passed a nurse on the street today
And she carried a bag like yours,
And on her wrist was a trinket chain
With an elephant and a horse,

155

I ran beside her and asked her where
She'd bought those silver charms,
But then she threatened to call the cops
And scream! - raise the alarm.

I have a terrible feeling, Ruth
But don't know who to tell,
And visions rise in my fevered brain
Of you in a makeshift hell,
Your kidneys sat in a freezer pack
Your liver and both of your eyes,
I asked for you at the hospital desk
But the nurse there told me lies.

I asked if you'd had an accident
Were lying in one of the wards,
She said, 'We never do accidents,
We'd just be swamped by the hordes.'
The place was run by a specialist
In transplants, great and small,
He had a long, continuous list
At a hundred grand a call.

The weeks have flown and you're still not home
So I watch, and stand outside,
And every patient that leaves the place
I look for your purple eyes,
They've got you listed as missing, girl
A poster on every pole,
But I know, whatever they find of you,
They're not going to get you whole.

The Body Snatchers

He peered on out at the darkening sky,
Pulled out the watch from its fob,
Traced his finger across the hand
That would time his nefarious job,
Then Matthew Scribbins packed his tools,
The short, strong wooden spade,
Designed for silence while biting deep
Into the dirt of the grave.

The wooden pushcart never came out
As long as the moon shone bright,
His lantern gave out a muted glow
That could barely be seen in the night,
The canvas sheeting lay in a roll
Ready to spread out wide,
To heap the dirt from his shovellings
Then wrap the body inside.

He took his orders from almoners
Watching the hospital wards,
They'd look for cadavers heading on out,
And tell him, 'This one is yours!'
Physicians needed a steady supply
For their students, fit to dissect,
The fresher the body the more it was worth
When he hauled it out by the neck.

He pushed his cart down the backyard lane
And whistled low for his youth,
Then out of the shadows crept his mark
An urchin called Henry Tooth,

For Henry went and he helped to dig
Or tunnelled from four feet down,
Then ripped the head from the coffin of deal
For the prize that was worth five pound.

'Tonight we've got us a lucky one,
Just buried this afternoon,
The earth is soft 'til the rains have come,
We'll be in and out in the gloom.'
He leered at Tooth as they pushed the cart
To the graveyard at Paxton Hurle,
'You 'll get a good look at what is what,
Tonight, we've got us a girl!'

The lad grinned back and he threw his cap
On the ground, and picked up the spade,
Went in at the head where the coffin was,
While the lantern lay in the shade,
In twenty minutes they hit the top
With a mute, dull muffled sound,
And smashed it through to attach the rope
Then pull the girl from the ground.

She lay with her eyes wide open there,
Looked blankly up at the sky,
Her hair in tresses around her neck
That said: 'It's a shame to die!'
Young Henry stared with a haunted look
And crossed himself in the dark,
'Get on with it boy, we haven't time,
We're not in a boating park!'

Then Scribbins caught at the hem of her shroud
And pulled it over her head,

She lay stark naked with pearly skin
In a stark affront to the dead,
They took the rings from her fingers then,
The earrings out of her ears,
And tossed them back in the coffin then
With the shroud, to banish their fears.

For theft was classed as a felony,
And that could have got them hung,
The body a misdemeanor, just
A fine or imprisonment.
They shovelled the earth back into the grave
And rolled the girl in the sheet,
Then placed her up on the handcart:
'Just imagine that she's asleep!'

They carried her to the dissection room
Picked up their pound of flesh,
Unrolled the girl on a marble slab,
The doctors would do the rest.
A novice thought he would make a cut
And raised a knife 'til it gleamed,
Her breast had quivered as he drew blood
And the girl sat up, and screamed!

Religicide

I *'must believe'* in something to be
Saved, so I've been told,
And practice all those rituals
Passed down from days of old,
Conform to thoughts conceived by men
Two thousand years ago,

The followers of Jesus, Buddha,
Krishna... So and so!

Then once I've made my choice I must
Resist all other faiths,
And war with each heretic, spill
Their blood, malign their race,
Aver that only my belief
Will take us to the stars,
While all those other foolish folk
Head to some place like Mars.

And all this on the words of those
Who trod the desert plains,
Who never saw an aeroplane,
Electric light or trains,
Knew nothing of the Internet
Or travel into space,
Who muttered superstitions round
The campfires of their race.

Our lives are fraught with peril as
Fanatics roam the earth,
Who seek to kill and maim us
By the values of their dearth,
No matter what I think, believe,
Or what man has begun,
The universe will plough its way
In circles, round the sun!

The Great Eastern

The bones of the great and troubled ship
Lay under a greying sky,
I'd travelled on up to Liverpool
To see the monster die,
The wreckers were ripping the hull apart,
Were opening wounds of old,
Not only the bones of a rusty ship
But the bones of a tale untold!

My mind went back those thirty years
To the time when we built the ship,
When I was a poor, young riveter,
Just out on my maiden trip,
I'd found some digs in Millwall,
Right down in the Isle of Dogs,
Where the Thames sweeps on forever
In a miasma of mist and fogs.

I moved on in with Ted and Jane,
The Lamptreys they were called,
He was a man of forty years,
She was just twenty four,
But Ted was grim and serious,
While Jane was as light as froth,
While he was around, he held her down,
I thought her a fluttering moth.

She'd laugh and dance, and prance around
When Ted was not at home,
He liked his pint of Guinness Stout,
His beer, a head of foam,

He said that he'd worked a mighty thirst
For Isambard Brunel,
Whose dream of the great Leviathan
Rose up from the depths of hell.

I got me a job with Ted down there,
Riveting iron plates,
That ship was the first with a double hull
With an inner working space,
We belted the red-hot rivets in
And flattened the ends across,
We'd work in pairs, and the light was scarce
In the depths of that albatross.

Whenever old Ted would seek the pub
I'd go on home to Jane,
I thought that she must have feelings,
But the love that I felt was pain,
For I never dared to voice it, though
She must have looked in my eyes,
To see the way that my feelings lay
It was way beyond disguise.

Then Ted had begun to drink too much,
He said it was getting him down,
All he could hear were the hammers,
Hammers, belting his head around.
They chimed all day in his weary head
They rang all night in his sleep,
Drowned out the sound of our laughter
Like an echo relayed from the deep.

He belted Jane and he made her cry
While I had nothing to say,

I thought that I couldn't come in-between
A man and his wife that way,
She saw my eyes, and they said it all,
I'd sit, and begin to grieve,
I just couldn't bear the thought that he
Might say that I had to leave!

The Eastern Company went bust,
Went broke in '56,
And we were all laid off, until
The finances were fixed,
We spent some terrible weeks at home,
Living on toast and tea,
Wondering how to pay the rent
And arguing constantly.

They hired us back, began again,
But Ted and I were sour,
For Jane had begun to talk to me,
Ignored him by the hour,
We worked down deep in the hull this time
But spoke not a friendly word,
With just the clash of the hammers as
The heat of our tempers soared.

He worked inside, in the inner space
As I beat the rivets in,
He'd disappear in the iron walls
To the clash of the hammer's din,
My mind began to play me tricks,
My hammer felt like lead,
And then as he peered on out one day,
I hit him across the head.

He fell back into that inner space
With neither a scream, nor curse,
I knew if I pulled him out again
There'd be calls for a horse and hearse.
I fitted a whole new iron plate
And riveted it in place,
Wiped the blood from my hammer,
And the sweat from my trembling face.

That night, I told poor Jane I'd left him
Outside the Crown and Heart,
She didn't say much 'til midnight when
He hadn't returned to the hearth,
For days, she hurried around to seek
Her husband in every lane,
But only I knew the reason why
He'd never come home again!

For months, I hoped and I prayed that
She would fall in my loving arms,
And weep her sorrows away with me
While sharing some of her charms.
But Jane was bitter and fretful, she
Would glare at me in the dark,
And nothing would raise her spirits now,
The light had gone from her spark.

The ship had neared completion when
I offered my hand to her,
'You must have guessed that I love you, Jane?'
She turned on me with a curse.
'You think to replace my husband? Hah!
I wouldn't take you on a whim,
For Ted was really my one true love,
I'll keep myself true to him!'

The ship was launched, and I left that place,
I signed as one of the crew,
I'd killed a man for a dream, like sand
That had trickled my fingers through.
I dreamt that Ted was alive, not dead
And clanking his length of chain,
In the bowels of Brunel's Great Eastern
And calling me out, by name!

That ship was cursed from the day it launched,
When one of the boilers blew,
As it crossed the Atlantic swell it lost
A paddle-wheel or two,
The rudder snapped at the iron post,
A reef put her in tow,
I knew full well that the hounds of hell
Were trapped there, down below!

I'm old and tired, as I watch the iron
Now stripped from the Eastern's side,
When suddenly there's a shout goes up:
'There's a skeleton inside!'
Now back in my lonely boarding house
I write this in despair,
In death, he waits with a hammer of hate,
Ted clanks his chains down there!

From God to Man

When we were numbered as old men
To peak, at three score years and ten,
God thought to have contained our pride,
As all our knowledge with us died.

But man was formed in God's own frame
And as such, he designed man's brain,
He must have known that what we knew
Would be passed on, from me to you.

And all the knowledge of God's mind
For generations, would unwind,
Would be recorded, pen and ink
And give descendants cause to think.

Our language would become refined
Beyond what he, in grace, designed,
Though he, in anger, rent the tower
Of Babel, man defied his power.

For science, in its infancy
Would lift his veil of secrecy,
Unravel every atom known
Of knowledge, that was God's alone.

'Til now, in pride and arrogance
Men say we happened here by chance,
There is no God up in the sky
But evolution brought us nigh!

Man is the ruler of his fate
We say, the lesson's learned too late
That man's corrupt, corroding hand
Wreaks pain and slaughter through the land.

And clever as men seem to claim
We can't control the falling rain,
We hide beneath our lightning rods,
But still men strut, and think they're Gods.

He sent the flood in times gone by
Then set his rainbow in the sky,
But if his covenant we break…
It may well be our last mistake!

Sandcastles

While sifting through old photographs
Of childhood, black and white,
I came across a scene that stirred
My memory, overnight,
Three children by a sandcastle,
The finest ever made,
My sister, me and Hazel,
Made with bucket, and with spade,
With towers, crenellations
And surrounded by a moat,
The sand was dry, the tide was out
It stood there proud, remote.

Though sixty years have passed since then,
That camera shutter's sight
Caught just one random moment in

An afternoon's delight,
It froze that moment of our lives,
That castle on the sand,
And though the tide swept in that day
That castle, still it stands,
While we watched as the sands of time
Wrought havoc in our lives,
The moat we built could not protect
From husbands, or from wives.

The tide swept in and filled the moat,
The sides began to melt,
The water undermined the walls
And suddenly, they fell,
The love that we had built them with
Was washed right out to sea,
And left no sign of love behind,
For Hazel, Tess or me,
And then we learned the lesson
That our lives revolved around,
That nothing built will last unless
It's built on solid ground.

We spent our lives in dreaming
Building castles in the sand,
Believing that the tide would never turn
To wreck our plans,
We thought love was the answer
'Til discovering, too late,
That love swings on a pendulum,
The other end is hate,
And just as tides flow in and out
And level out the land,
The tides of life wreak havoc with
Our castles in the sand.

The Attic

'There's nobody in
But the light is on
And a chair just creaked,
Did you hear it, son?
There's been no chairs
For ever so long,
So who's abroad
In the attic, son?'

'That grim old lady
Who haunts the stairs
In a faded dress
With a world of cares,
Whenever I look
She disappears,
But lives in a world
That's drowned in tears.'

'They say she mutters
Beneath the moon
From the window there
In the month of June,
The light was out
In that ancient room
When she jumped from the window,
Into the gloom.'

'Why does she haunt
The attic, son,
If her soul took flight
When the moon was gone?

What is she trying
To tell us, son?'

'There's nobody in
But the light is on!'

Death's Call

I heard my friend died yesterday,
It knocked me off my feet,
I'd passed the time of day with him
Last Wednesday, on the street,
He'd caught me at an awkward time,
I strained to get away,
He had some awful flu, or cold,
I didn't want to stay.

He phoned me later, chatted on,
I looked up at the sky,
I'm always so impatient with
This one annoying guy,
His jokes were inappropriate,
He laughed at them himself,
When wit was handed out, they left
His sitting on the shelf.

He wrote a bit, of prose and verse,
It wasn't up to scratch,
I'd see him coming up the drive
And flick across the latch,
He'd want me to critique them
And I'd hate to lay him low,

By telling him his talent was
Not up to 'so and so'.

He seemed to think that I was
Someone special in his life,
And tried to join the family
By chatting up my wife,
He really thought I didn't know
But still I kept my peace,
I didn't tell his wife on him,
Or tear him off a piece.

The one thing I will say is that
He always had a smile,
Whenever he caught up with me,
With notepad, book or file,
I've never known one try so hard
For friendship, in despair,
And in return, I'd tell the wife
'Just keep him out my hair!'

But now he's dead, so suddenly,
It's time that I took stock,
The friendship was all his, you see,
And all I did was block.
The fault was not in him, I see,
But in my tardy soul,
For he deserved much more than me,
And now, I'm feeling old.

I wasted all the chances that
He offered me, for free,
To just enjoy a simple soul,
One who looked up to me.

I'm going to miss that little man
And pray his soul to keep,
For now I'd welcome anyone
To talk to, in the street!

The Church of Wenslow Haze

The sea that batters the eastern coast
Has often subdued the land,
Five hundred years have seen the retreat
Of a mile of cliffs and sand,
When tides are low in the summertime
From beneath the distant swell,
The villagers lying abed at night
Hear the tolling of a bell.

The bell resounds up the village street
And rattles the cobblestones,
As the villagers close the shutters tight
And lock the doors of their homes,
They hear the sound of a wooden stump
As it echoes along the street,
The wooden leg of the mate, John Clegg
From Drake's Armada Fleet!

The thump is steady and purposeful
As it heads towards the sea,
Where the bell still rings for matins
As in 1563,
When priests were burned for popery
In the England of those days,
They used the little singing cakes
In the Church of Wenslow Haze!

John Clegg was a surly protestant
In the service of the Queen,
So the use of the cakes for massing bread -
He thought it was quite obscene!
The vicar had leant to the Roman Church,
The Reverend Walter Raise,
And Clegg had stood and harangued him there
In the Church of Wenslow Haze.

'You'll bring your Popish habits here
At the risk of mortal pain,
I fought for the Queen Elizabeth
To see off the King of Spain,
If you don't revert to the massing bread
And the Book of Common Prayer,
I'll see to the piling of faggots
When they burn you in the square!'

But Walter Raise would never be stayed
By the threats of an ignorant tar,
He said: 'I only answer to God
For the what and the where we are!
The form is not as important as
The salving of the soul,
You'd better look to your own before
The Devil takes you all!'

But Clegg had waited for matins, he
Returned with a burning brand,
Set fire to the ancient tapestries
The pews and the altar stand,
He raised his cutlass and brought it down
On the Romish vicar's head,

And he cursed the Church of Wenslow Haze
As the vicar lay there, dead!

The sea rose up in a sudden storm
And it swept across the land,
Engulfed the Church of Wenslow Haze
As if raised by God's own hand,
The land had tilted beneath the sea
And the church, it settled deep,
With the bodies of Clegg and Walter Raise
And the bell-tower, and the keep!

So now when the tide repents and drops
To a fathom, over the bell,
The toll rings out from the surly deep
Like a call to the fiends from hell,
And a stump sounds over the cobblestones
As Clegg, for his soul's sake pays,
He carries a burning fire brand
To the Church of Wenslow Haze.

Oradour-sur-Glane

I woke to the smell of new baked bread
From the bakery, down the way,
Mama was singing and feeding the hens,
I had no school today,
Pierre and I had arranged to go
For a ramble, soon or late,
To look for the trilling skylark's nest,
And the hedgehog's rolling gait.

Papa was sat in the garden, he
Was fixing my sister's bike,
While Grandpa sat on the old wood bench,
Filling his gnarled old pipe,
The sun was set in a pale blue sky
And the lord smiled down on the town,
The war was a million miles away
From Oradour-sur-Glane.

Pierre was waiting across the street,
We ran with a whoop of joy,
'I'll race you out to the barley field,'
He said, my cousin's boy.
We found a hollow within the crop
Lay there in the broad sunlight,
And watched the birds as they swooped on down
From their laughing, joyous flight!

At two o'clock, we heard the clatter
Of many an Army truck,
They drove to surround the village fields,
There were twenty, near enough.

Then soldiers leapt from the canopies,
Their uniforms were black,
An SS sign on their collars, and
A skull on each forage cap!

They herded the workers into the town,
We lay in a funk, and hid,
We heard the guttural, sharp commands,
They did as the soldiers bid,
A woman ran in a terror then,
A shot rang out and she fell,
Pierre stood up, as he ran he cried:
'That was my aunt Giselle!'

I said: 'Come back!' but he ran towards
The centre of the town,
A shot rang out as he scaled the fence,
Pierre went tumbling down!
I knew at once that my friend was dead,
I held my breath, and wept,
And burrowed deep in the barley field,
I see his body yet!

They marched the men en masse along
To Madame Laudy's barn,
They led the women and children
To the church, in their alarm!
They took the babies, pushers too,
Crammed deep inside the church,
But then the SS opened fire,
And they lit a blazing torch.

The men, they were slaughtered in the barn,
They never told them why,

The barn went up in flames as well,
I lay in the field, and cried,
I lost my mother and sister too,
My father and my gran,
The Devil smiled on his work that day
In Oradour-sur Glane!

They burnt the town, burnt every home,
They turned the town to hell,
I wonder whether the soldiers wept
When they went down, as well;
For off the coast, at Normandy
Was an Army with a plan,
To slay the butchers that killed the town
Of Oradour-sur-Glane!

The Farmer's Wife

'Why the commotion now, my love?
You cry at the breaking dawn,
The dog's asleep in his kennel still
Though the cock has crowed for the morn;
The birds have stirred in the branches there
Of the willow, out by the lake,
Why do you weep, and cry, and mourn
Before you're even awake?'

'What became of the silence we
Enjoyed in the days gone by,
When a simple glance was enough romance
And we lay, looked up at the sky.
When a whispered word that I barely heard
Would sound from your own sweet lips,

As my hand reached out to relieve your doubt,
Caressing your fingertips?'

'I must get out to the barley field,
The sheep are starting to lamb,
The fence is down by the hillside mound,
And the water's leached from the dam,
The days are long, and I must be strong
For the work will never keep,
So why do you lie and weep and cry
When I need to get to sleep?'

'The pigs broke out of the pen last night,
I must rebuild the sty,
They're wandering over the cabbage patch,
So today, it's do or die!
I haven't the help I used to have
Since John – well! I should have said,
He toppled the tractor in the ditch
And now, well now, he's dead!'

'Nothing will bring him back you know,
Your crying's all in vain,
All of those hours he spent with you
They caused me only pain!
Settle your head and love me now
As once you did in the past…'
'Never!' she said, her eyes were dead
And the tears came thick and fast!

Black Gold

The Dad was dour, his face was sour
When he came home from the pit,
He looked like a furnace stoker but
That wasn't the half of it…
His fists were like a couple of hams
And he used the blighters, too,
The Mam would hear his foot on the step
And hurry to serve his stew.

She wore his bruises over her face,
Her arms and her legs and more,
I'd seen her body all over then
For I was coming-up four,
I'd watched the blood run down her leg
As she cleaned herself with a rag,
Whenever he'd come home roaring drunk,
Use Mam as a punching bag!

My sister Else was barely ten
When he made her work at the pit,
She struggled to push a cart of coal
Until she was almost sick.
The manager was a brutal man
With a knotted, leather strap,
If Else was slow or got vertigo
He'd lay it across her back!

I never heard Mam complain to him,
I guess that she didn't dare,
She'd rub some cream into Else's wounds
And run a brush through her hair.

'It's hard, but you'll toughen up, my girl,
He said, as a sort of scold,
'You'd better respect what we're mining here,
Just think of it as Black Gold!'

'Think of it as Black Gold,' he'd said…
(The sort that gets into your pores,
The dust that gives you a crippled lung
And your skin gets covered in sores.
The cough that's keeping the house awake
When everyone needs to sleep,
The sulphur smell round the chimney-piece
As you watch your mother weep!)

He dragged me out, and he took me in
When I was only eight,
He said, 'Now look here, fella-me-lad,
It's time that you pulled your weight!'
They started me at tuppence a day
And sat me down in the shaft,
I had to open and close a trap
To help to create the draught.

The hours were long, the days were long
We worked a twelve hour shift,
It took me an hour to get to the face,
Clambering over the drift,
I didn't get time to go to school,
Still sign my name with an 'x',
But I'm learning now at the Institute
Just to try for a little respect!

When I was ten, they sent me down
With a pick to the old coal face,

Where miners hammered and banged like hell
And they tried to make me race,
Poor Else, still pushing the trucks of coal,
Her back had formed in a hump,
The boys would whistle and jeer at her
For her legs were like two stumps.

New-fangled ships were coming in,
The ones of steel and steam,
'It's only good for the working man,'
The Dad said: 'Good for the team!'
But some of the stopes were caving in
The mine was in full retreat,
We'd pull what pillars of coal were left
And send them up to the street.

The Dad was working the furthest pitch
While Else sat crippled and old,
She'd ripped a tendon and looked quite lost
As she sat by a pillar of coal,
She waved me away to the further stope
And attacked the coal with a pick,
The pillar came suddenly crashing down
And the roof - it followed it!

I never saw Mam cry for The Dad,
She cried for our Else instead,
'She never had much of a life at all,
I'm glad the old bugger's dead!'
Now the years have passed, and I understand
That The Dad was true to his kind,
He never had much of a chance at all
And he's buried, still in the mine!

Panzer

Gretchen wept in her easy chair
And called for her husband, Karl,
They'd been together for sixty years,
Though both were worn and frail.
They'd met in the ruins of München, when
The Reich collapsed and fell,
Escaped to live in Australia
From their own idea of hell.

For Karl had served in the Wermacht,
In a Tank Corps at Dieppe,
Had served in the Panzergruppe von Kleist
Had roamed the Russian steppes,
His tank had taken him through Ukraine
They'd taken the plains by force,
But found their pain when the Russians came,
In their huge T-34's.

But that was the world of way back when,
For Karl was old and grey,
He slept a lot in his tidy home,
The nurse came every day,
His wife developed dementia, she'd
Forget where she used to roam,
So she was parted from husband Karl,
Was sent to a Nursing Home!

He walked with the aid of a walking frame,
He couldn't quite get around,
But listened for echoes of Gretchen's voice
In the house that made no sound,

And all he thought was to rescue her,
To bring his girl back home,
But the powers that be said: 'Wait and see!'
She was lost to him - Alone!

He went to visit her, once a week,
They held each other's hand,
She cried so much when he had to leave,
She never could understand,
And he was desolate every time,
He'd cling to her so tight,
That they had to prise his hand away
When they sent him away at night.

The nurses were harsh and businesslike,
To them it was just a job,
With no compassion for patients, they
Would leave all that to God.
Demented souls ran over his feet
With trolleys and walking frames,
When Karl grew angry, they shrugged and said:
'Well - Everyone complains!'

One Sunday, standing outside the doors,
He saw his Tiger Tank,
It growled, and pulled up beside him there
And the diesel fumes, they stank.
He climbed aboard with his comrades there,
And 'Schnell!' they called, to a man,
Then lumbered straight through the double doors,
The nurses turned and ran!

The Tiger reared and it turned about
Tore carpet up from the floor,

The tracks ran over the matron's feet,
Let out a fearful roar,
The patients cheered as the Iron Cross
Raced past their common room,
And smashed the glass in the office door,
And crushed the sister's urn!

Then Gretchen laughed as he came in sight,
'Here comes my husband, Karl!
He'll break us out of this prison ward,
Can you hear his Tiger snarl?'
He stopped and reached for his Gretchen then
Looked deep in her eyes, and swore:
'I'll not be parted from you again
Though hell should bar the door!'

They found them lying together there,
He held her safe in his arms,
They'd gone together where lovers go
Away from the world's alarms.
'He went quite crazy,' the Matron said,
'He must have been insane!'
For lying outside her shattered door
Was his twisted walking frame!

No Man's Land

I'd been cleaning out the attic
And the gables in the roof,
Which were dusty, full of cobwebs
And a horror, tell the truth,
There were boxes, wooden chests
And mouldy papers overall,
'Til the ceiling couldn't take it,
It was bowed, about to fall.

So we shunted all this detritus
Until it filled the space
We had cleared on the landing
To gain access to the place,
'What on earth are we to do with it?'
My wife said in despair,
'We'll have to burn the lot,' I said,
'Except that old box chair.'

I remembered the old box chair
From my Grandad's, Arthur Oates,
It was taken from a hallstand
Where we'd hung our hats and coats,
It was made of polished oak, and sat
So proudly, just inside,
My father must have brought it home
When my Grandfather died.

Later, when we'd finished sorting,
Burning, and so on,
I lifted up the lid to see
What treasures I had won,

My gas mask from the second war
That looked like Mickey Mouse,
Was sitting still within that box,
So many years had passed.

I tipped out scarves and ancient gloves
That still lay buried there,
My sister's broken China Doll
The type that had no hair,
And at the bottom, going brown
And brittle, somewhat dank,
My Grandad's faded diary,
With Number, Name and Rank.

I read it through that very night,
I sat there in the gloom,
And there the 'War to End all Wars'
Unfolded in my room,
It left me pensive, sitting there
For now I understood,
Those many journeys made to France,
My Grandad's bitter moods.

In 1914, Christmastime
He'd lain there in his trench,
The ground was hard and white that morn,
The atmosphere was tense,
The Germans in their trenches were
Just fifty yards away,
He heard them bursting into song,
They Carolled forth that day.

The strip that they called 'No Man's Land'
Lay under recent snow,

The bodies of the slain lay there,
No Christmas would they know!
A note came from the German side
A ceasefire, honour pledged,
Allowing each to venture out
Unharmed, bury their dead.

My grandfather had watched in awe
As slowly, German heads,
Rose up above their parapets,
Dispersed their fear and dread,
He climbed on out himself, and wandered
Over No Man's Land,
When the advancing Boche had smiled,
He shook a German's hand.

They wished a Merry Christmas each
These soldiers who were foes,
They were just men in uniforms
That day, as Jesus knows,
'We have no wish to kill you now,'
One said, 'nor you kill us,
So why shoot on this Christmas Day,
I'm you – you're one of us!'

They all exchanged small gifts that day,
Cigars, chocolate, tobacco,
They spoke in English, and in French
In accents loud, staccato,
They laughed and joked and passed around
Snapshots, from hand to hand,
They even played scratch football
Cheered and laughed, in No Man's Land.

My grandfather then wrote at length
Of one young lad, a Hun,
Blonde haired, blued eyed, his name was Franz
He seemed a friendly one,
They promised, they would find each other
When the war was done,
And drink to peace with Schnapps and Gin,
Scotch Whiskey, one for one.

That day the guns lay silent, then
They filed back to each trench,
Cat-called and whistled, bandied jokes,
Those soldiers were just men,
At midnight the ceasefire was off,
They all fired in the air,
No-one was hitting anyone
Across that land – 'Despair!'

But then the 'War to End all Wars'
Went grimly back on course,
The Officers made threats, and soon
Their orders lent them force,
My grandfather fired at a head
That bobbed in No Man's Land,
The Boche had fallen dead before
He recognised him - Franz.

I always thought my grandfather
Was grim, there was no light,
That animated him by day,
Or cheered his soul by night,
He spoke just once about the war
And said – 'War should be banned!
You'll never understand the horror,
There, in No Man's Land.'

Dunkirk

They came from a line of fishermen,
Way back, two hundred years,
The sons of a dour old Kentish man,
Who'd braved the First World War;
When Joe went off to the Army, then,
The old man's face was grim,
'You go and fight for the country, lad,
We can't rely on him!'

He scowled on down at the eldest lad
Who sat there, mending nets,
For all he knew was the salt, the sea
And a life of cheap regrets.
The black sheep of the family
Was all that his father saw,
For Jack had refused the Army call:
'I don't believe in war!'

A feather came in the post next day,
As white as a cotton sheet,
The father turned his back on him
For shame, and refused to speak.
While Joe went off with the B.E.F.
To help the beleaguered French,
Jack was mending his fishing nets,
And sat with his fingers clenched.

Their fishing boat, the Pelican,
Lay stranded in Sandwich Bay,
Just twenty feet, and clinker built,
With the deckhouse cut away.

189

When the Panzers swept down to the coast,
Reaching the channel first,
The B.E.F. had retreated back
To the beaches at Dunkirk.

The Navy sent destroyers then,
Their frigates and corvettes,
But couldn't get close to the beaches there
Because of the shallow depths,
The Navy's own small vessel pool
Then called for the help of those
Whose boats were a certain shallow draught
To ferry the soldiers home.

When Jack came in, the news was out,
His mother sat, dismayed,
The Army was stranded along the beach
Where Joe lay low, and prayed.
The Stuka's screamed, and dropped their bombs
And the lines of men were strafed,
Three hundred thousand men despaired
As the Panzers lay in wait.

'So much for you,' the father said,
As the tears poured down his cheek,
'So much for the lunacy of war,'
Said Jack, when he could speak.
'Your brother's out there, risking all,
My son, my shining light!'
But Jack stalked out with a bitter laugh,
And cried, once out of sight.

He strode on out to the Pelican,
The tide was coming in,

He dragged and pushed it to meet the sea
As he floated it again,
He kicked the inboard into life
And he sailed for Ramsgate then,
The boats were gathering by the score
To save their countrymen.

They sailed that night in convoys, groups,
And lines of little boats,
While Jack prayed long at the tiller
That the Pelican stayed afloat,
She'd never been out as far as this,
She was just a coastal craft…
But Joe stood out in the water, then,
And thought of his brother, Jack.

The Stuka's bombed the Naval ships,
They strafed the lines of men,
Joe didn't know if he'd ever get back
To his homeland, once again.
The Foudroyant was bombed and sank,
A destroyer ran aground,
Then a hundred boats with the Pelican,
Finally sighted land.

Jack took the Pelican close inshore
And he loaded his twenty men,
He ferried them out to a waiting ship
Then turned to the shore again,
He plucked the men from the waters there
And he looked for his brother Joe,
But Joe was safe on a steamer, then,
Though his brother didn't know.

For hours he turned, and turned about,
He saved five hundred lives,
He worked himself to exhaustion there
Like a man who the devil drives,
Eight hundred ships and boats were there
In the smoke and the swirling murk,
To bring those thousands of soldiers home
From the beaches of Dunkirk.

Joe walked unsteadily through the door
To the cries of his folks, alone,
They couldn't speak for the pure relief
Of seeing him safe at home,
But his father suddenly pulled away,
And wept, while turning his back,
'We've just been told by the foot patrol…
We've lost your brother, Jack!'

'They said the Pelican's hull was holed
With a burst of cannon rounds,
The men on board were saved, I heard,
But three of them were drowned.
They left the bodies to float out there;
Oh God; now, what have I done?'
He shook his head as he cried, and said,
'I've lost my eldest son!'

They placed a plaque on the Harbour wall
For Jack and the Pelican,
While the father stared most days to sea
As he cried there, off and on,
Then he took a match and some tinder wood
For a pledge he'd made before,
To burn a pure white feather there
For a son who hated war.

One by One...

If I should disappear one sudden night,
Escape, take flight, cast off my chains
And venture out one final time
Into the darkening light,
To leave this sinking hulk behind
Mired fast in weeds, and shallow deeds
That never now may be undone;
Take heed, I pray, who loved me once –
Death takes us, one by one!

If once you speak, but never get reply,
Though my eyes stare, not having said goodbye
When all that moved me, once, has gone
To join in common history the fate of everyman…
Don't cry for me, for I am well content;
A life, lived, loved, and now made more complete
By ending thus, as everything must end.
No - save your tears for those I leave behind,
Grief is for the living, not the dead and blind!

And if you need some final words from me
To give you hope, some ultimate destiny,
As each one passes from this mortal stage, I say
'Have faith!' - as you, too, approach the end of days.
Be calm, accept, and we shall all be saved,
Just as the servant, taking back the keys of life
Confronts the Master he has served, in every faith,
And hears the words: 'My son, you've done us proud!'
Gives back the key, and takes from him the shroud.

www.ingramcontent.com/pod-product-compliance
Lightning Source LLC
LaVergne TN
LVHW051631080426
835511LV00016B/2284